WHAT ECONOMISTS DO:
A JOURNEY THROUGH THE HISTORY OF
ECONOMIC
THOUGHT

WHAT ECONOMISTS DO:
A JOURNEY THROUGH THE HISTORY OF
ECONOMIC
THOUGHT
FROM THE WEALTH OF NATIONS TO THE CALCULUS OF CONSENT

ATTIAT F. OTT, WITH SHEILA VEGARI

iUniverse LLC
Bloomington

What Economists Do: A Journey through the History of Economic Thought From the Wealth of Nations to the Calculus of Consent

iUniverse books may be ordered through booksellers or by contacting:

iUniverse LLC
1663 Liberty Drive
Bloomington, IN 47403
www.iuniverse.com
1-800-Authors (1-800-288-4677)

Because of the dynamic nature of the Internet, any web addresses or links contained in this book may have changed since publication and may no longer be valid. The views expressed in this work are solely those of the author and do not necessarily reflect the views of the publisher, and the publisher hereby disclaims any responsibility for them.

Any people depicted in stock imagery provided by Thinkstock are models, and such images are being used for illustrative purposes only.
Certain stock imagery © Thinkstock.

ISBN: 978-1-4917-0126-3 (sc)
ISBN: 978-1-4917-0128-7 (hc)
ISBN: 978-1-4917-0127-0 (ebk)

Library of Congress Control Number: 2013914081

Printed in the United States of America

iUniverse rev. date: 08/08/2013

CONTENTS

To Dr. William Blake (1924-2012), my physician and friend,
who inspired me to write this book.

PREFACE

In this volume I address a question that was raised in an old movie run by Turner Classic Movies a few months ago: What do economists do? The question attracted my attention, although I neither knew what film it was from, nor who raised it. At first, I shrugged off the question and went about my business, but the question did not go away. I decided to run an experiment, albeit with a small sample. I asked few of my former PhD students in economics at Clark University the same question. Well, we did not exactly generate a simple or satisfactory answer. I knew then that I would have to dig deeper to find out a satisfactory answer to the query.

In addressing what economists do, my initial thought was to compare economist with other professional labels, such as doctor, pharmacist, lawyer, and so on. This approach did not pan out for the simple reason that such occupations have a very well defined spaces, clients, and outcomes. The next comparison was with similar occupations—political scientists, sociologists, and the like. This comparison did not help much either, as economics is but one strand of social science. The answer would have to be found elsewhere: in a journey through the history of economic thought.

Going through my bookshelves I dusted off eighteenth—and nineteenth-century books dealing mostly with principles of economics. To complete the journey, I have selected few somewhat modern texts from the twentieth century, so that a continuum of economic ideas can be captured.

In such an endeavor, one has to be selective. The authors I have selected clearly reflect my own biases, but my choices were influenced most of all by the time constraint that every writer faces. Thus, I have limited the selection to the contributions of nine writers: Adam Smith (1776), Thomas Robert Malthus (1798), David Ricardo (1817), John Stuart Mill (1848), Leon Walras (1873, 1876), John Maynard Keynes (1936), Richard A. Musgrave (1955), James Buchanan and Gordon Tullock (1965), and Paul A. Samuelson (1966). Missing from this list are so many writers who were critical in shaping the discipline. Clearly Joseph Schumpeter, Fredric Hayek, and Milton Friedman are among those who have revolutionized their fellow economists' thinking and their teaching of economics.

It is to be understood from the outset that the objective of the research, was not to provide a review of all the themes or doctrines advanced by the economists selected. Rather, it was to put forth their views on three issues: first, the subject and principles of economics; second, economics as a science, and third, the function of the economist.

The selection process is clearly subject to several limitations, but most of all it reflects my own biases and interests as well as an inherent time constraint. Nonetheless, I believe that the thesis and ideas presented offer the reader an interesting and worthwhile look at the founders and the foundations of the discipline of economics. Most of all, it paints an intriguing picture of how economics have come of age and become a distinct body of knowledge.

This search ultimately provided me with the answer to the question: What do economists do? The search identified for us the first person on whom the title of "economist" was bestowed upon. Paul Samuelson, a Nobel Laureate in Economics (1970), named Adam Smith the "first" economist, and no one in the economic profession is likely to disagree.

In writing this volume, I have discussed the subject matter and my selection of contributors with two of my former students at Clark University, Drs. Bonnie Orcutt and Sheila Vegari. As I undertook the journey through the history of economic thought, Dr. Vegari was interested to see how my journey would address the question of what economists do. In the course of my research, I have benefited greatly from her suggestions.

Acknowledgments are also due to Drs. Orcutt and Vlad Dologopolov for their enthusiastic support for undertaking this venture. Drs. Michael Johnson and Oswaldo Patino provided support in the development of the manuscript. Special thanks go to the iUniverse reviewer and editor for their valuable comments and suggestions.

The volume is organized as follows: Chapter 2 offers an essay on the subject of economics; chapter 3 reviews some of the arguments presented about economics as a science. Chapter 4 presents principles of political economy. There the subject of inquiry is limited to microeconomic principles. This is followed in chapter 5 by the principles of the macro economy as put forth by John Maynard Keynes in *The General Theory*. Of note is the division of the body of knowledge in the discipline of economics into microeconomics and macroeconomics. Whereas macroeconomics deals with the determination of national output (income), employment, inflation, and interest rates, microeconomics explains the determination of market prices, individuals' consumption choices, and labor supply. Next, in chapter 6 the analysis presented covers the principles of the public economy set forth by the classical economists augmented by the work of Paul Samuelson and Richard Musgrave. The public choice school developed by James Buchanan and Gordon Tullock places the public economy and its structure in a different perspective from the one offered by the classical economists and the contribution to it that was made by Samuelson and Musgrave. Their analyses, presented in this chapter, although condensed and simplified, conclude the chapter. Chapter 7 addresses the question "What do economists do?" by examining the role of the economist as a teacher, a political economist, and as an adviser to policy makers. The final chapter, Chapter 8 is the conclusion.

Attiat F. Ott

CHRONICLE OF ECONOMIC HISTORY

Adam Smith (1776): An inquiry into The Wealth of Nations, First Edition, The Modern Library, Random House, Inc
> "Political economy considered as a branch of the science of a statesman or legislator, proposes two distinct objects: first to provide a plentiful revenue or subsistence for the people, or more properly to enable them to provide such a revenue or subsistence for themselves, and secondly, to supply the state or commonwealth with revenue sufficient for the public services. It proposes to enrich both the people and the sovereign."

Robert. Malthus (1798): On Population. Edited by Gertrude Himmelfarb, The Modern Library, New York, 1960.
> "The course which has the most lasting effect in improving the situation of the lower classes of society depends chiefly upon the conduct and prudence of the individuals than on the sovereign."

David Ricardo (1817): The Works and Correspondence of David Ricardo, edited by Pierosraffa with the collaboration of M.H. Dobb, vol1, On The Principles of Political Economy and Taxation, published by Cambridge University Press, 1952.
> "The problem of the earth . . . all that is derived from the surface by the united application of labor, machinery, and capital is divided among three classes of the community; namely the proprietors of the land, the owner

of the stock of capital necessary for the cultivation, and the labourers by whose industry it is cultivated . . . to determine the laws which regulate this distribution is the principal problem in political economy."

John Stuart Mill (1848): Principles of Political Economy, With Some of Their Applications to Social Philosophy. Edited with an introduction by Sir William Ashley, reprint of economic classics, new edition (1909) Published by Augustus M. Kelley Publishers, New York, New York, 1969.

"Mankind, individually or collectively, can do with wealth as they please, and on whatever terms—even what a person has produced by his individual toil—not only can society take it from him, but individuals could and would if society did not—the distribution of wealth, therefore, depends on the laws and customs of society."

Leon Walras (1873-1876): Elements of Pure Economics, translated by William Jaffee. First Edition published in 1874 and 1877 in two installments, 1954.

"The sum total of all things, material or immaterial, on which a price can be set because they are scarce, constitutes social wealth. Hence, pure economics is also the theory of social wealth."

Alfred Marshall (1890): Principles of Economics: An Introductory Volume. London: Macmillan and Co. Limited, 1948.

"Economics is a study of mankind in the ordinary business of life, it examines that part of individual and social action which is most clearly connected with attainment and with the use of the material requisites of well being. Thus it is both a study of wealth and study of man."

John Maynard Keynes (1936): The General Theory of Employment, Interest and Money, London, Macmillan and Co. Ltd 1954

"The ideas of economists and political philosophers both when they are right and when they are wrong are more powerful than is commonly understood. Indeed, the world is ruled by little else."

Richard Able Musgrave (1959): The Theory of Public Finance: A Study of Public Economics, McGraw Hill Book Company
"Intelligent conduct of government requires an understanding of the economic relations and the economist, by aiding in this understanding, may hope to contribute to a better society."

James M. Buchanan and Gordon Tullock (1965): The Calculus of Consent; Logical Foundations of Constitutional Democracy, Ann Arbor Paper Books, The University of Michigan Press
"Is there a logical economic rationalization or explanation for the emergence of democratic political institutions? On the basis of our individualistic assumptions about human motivations can we "explain" the adoption of political constitution."

Paul A. Samuelson (1966): The Collected Scientific Papers of P. A. Samuelson, vol. 2, edited by Joseph Stiglitz. Book Five, Cambridge, MA, The MIT Press.
"If economists spend more and more of their time on highly technical mathematics and statistics they must not be surprised if the intelligent man of affairs comes to ignore this part of their activities."

1 INTRODUCTION

This volume seeks to provide insight about the role of economists. In order to do so, it is necessary that we clearly define our subject, in other words, what the discipline is all about. A journey through the history of economic thought will unlock the doors to not only what economists actually do but also what economics is all about.

To provide you with this insight, I have put forth those ideas and principles advanced by the forefathers of what has become known as economics. Back in the seventeenth, eighteenth centuries, and even in the nineteenth century, economics, or more accurately political economy, dealt with many issues that face societies today, from the raising of revenues for the sovereign (the state) and the allocation of the tax burden, to protection of local industry and free trade. The principles put forth by early writers laid the foundation of what we know today as economics. To be sure, the discipline of economics has undergone a great deal of change, yet the questions it deals with have remained the same. One of which is what constitutes the wealth of the nation.

The journey to defining the wealth of a nation takes us to the first economist, Adam Smith. Many readers will be familiar with Adam Smith's reference to the "invisible hand". But in what context did Smith put forth such an idea. Our journey helps to put Smith's famous phrase in context. Smith's other seldom-discussed ideas relate to the function of the government, including the provision of public goods, especially education and national defense, as well as his warnings about the unbridled power of captains of industry.

Besides Adam Smith, the political economists of the eighteenth and nineteenth century who are credited for laying down the foundations of political economy include David Ricardo, John Stuart Mill, and Alfred Marshall; they helped make a home for the economist.

Although the principles of economics put forth in this volume give a clear view of the origins of the discipline, they do not encompass the entire body of knowledge advanced by the economists we have selected. To do so would have required a different type of book, one which would undoubtedly attract a different audience. What we have selected, though limited in scope, nonetheless gives answers about the discipline and economists generally. Moreover, by including in the journey the most notable economists of the twentieth century—John Maynard Keynes, Paul Samuelson, Richard Musgrave, James Buchanan and Gordon Tullock—it becomes clear why economic policies in the United States as well as the majority of countries in the world heed the advice of economists, even though they may not always be "right".

2   THE SUBJECT OF ECONOMICS

"The Main Concern of Economics is thus with Human Being who are Impelled for Good or evil, to Change and Progress"

(Marshall, *Principles of Economics in the Preface to the First Edition*).

Definitions

Economics is the study of the fundamentals governing the activities of individuals, businesses, and governments. The tools of analysis have been shaped over time not by one but by all these entities.

If you were to ask an undergraduate student enrolled in an introductory course in economics, "What is the subject of economics?" You are likely to hear one of two things: "economics is the study of supply and demand" or that it is the "study of the economy". Of course both of these answers are correct, and one cannot fault the student for falling back on what a textbook in economics or instructors teach about economics in the classroom. Two popular textbooks in economics that were used in many introductory courses in economics are those of Edwin Mansfield (*Economics*, 1974) and Nicholas and Reynolds (*Principles of Economics*, 1971). Both texts, as well as many others, introduced the subject matter in the preface or the first two chapters of their book.

Mansfield, sought to introduce the subject by alluding to what a student is likely to expect: the use of society resources. According to

Mansfield, "economics is concerned with the way society's resources are allocated among alternative uses to satisfy human wants" (Chapter 1, p.1). Mansfield however did not think that such a definition was useful as it was loaded with vague terms such as "resources" and "wants". Thus, he advanced an alternative definition, which suggests that one can better ascertain what economics is about by looking at the "problems" economics helps to solve.

In the preface to their volume, Nicholas and Reynolds posit that economics is "a cohesive body of thought that is felt to be a useful way of looking at many different problems". The problem that economics will have to solve is the "distribution of material satisfaction among the society's members". Defining economics as a body of knowledge that is capable of solving society's problem of resource scarcity gives economics much more than it can truly deliver.

The history of economic thought presents us with a muddled picture about the subject of economics. Before putting down who said what, it is to be emphasized from the outset that early writers were not of one mind about what constitutes the subject. Economics, or political economy, was not developed from its inception as a cohesive body of knowledge; rather it developed piecemeal to address problems of the time. The publication of Adam Smith's *Inquiry into the Nature and Causes of the Wealth of Nations* in 1789 changed the scene by providing the foundations of the discipline we now refer to as economics.

A definition of what the subject of economics entails was neither needed for Smith's book to make its mark on what has become to be known as economics, nor for the success of Alfred Marshall's *Principles of Economics*, published in 1890. The issue confronting the writers of this era was not one of definition but rather of what the "science" has to offer. Smith wrote:

> Political Economy, considered as a branch of the science of a statesman or the legislator, proposes two distinct objects: First, to provide plentiful revenue or subsistence for the people, or more properly enable them to provide such a revenue or subsistence for themselves, and secondly to supply the state or commonwealth with a revenue sufficient for public services (Smith 1776, 1937 Ed, p.397).

4

This definition outlines the problem as one of distribution of society's resources between the private and the public sectors. Of note is that Smith treats economics as a branch of science, a particular science that is of service to the legislator (the government); that it defines the function the legislator is supposed to perform; and that for such a service the legislator is entitled to compensation. Given that the legislator is to be compensated for his efforts, Smith opened the door for the legislator to secure those resources that would be needed to provide "public services".

Alfred Marshall is more prolific in addressing the subject of economics. Marshall was of the view that one definition would not convey all. In his *Principles of Economics*, Marshall defines economics as a "study of men as they live and move and think in the ordinary business of life. But it concerns itself chiefly with those motives, which affect, most powerfully and most steadily, man's conduct in the business part of life" (chapter 11, p.14, 1948 Ed). Marshall outlined how economics view man—"a man who is largely influenced by egotistic motives in his business life" (p.20). Economics, according to Marshall, deals with "facts" which can be observed and quantities that can be measured. He refines further the definition by stating that "the business of economics, as almost every other science, is to collect facts, to arrange and interpret them and to draw inferences from them" (p.29).

Walras, in his *Elements of Political Economy* (1800s), devoted his first lesson to reason out what economics or political economy is by surveying the literature of the time, including the writing of Quesnay and his disciples of the "Physiocrat" school (Quesnay 1758), Adam Smith (1780), Robert Malthus (1817) and J. B. Say (1803). None of these authors' definitions seem to satisfy him. In effect, he was critical of all, but reserved his harshest critique for J. B. Say.

Walras went about looking for a definition that conveyed what the "science" of economics was about. Apologetically he wrote: "I have not thought of evading my obligation for offering a definition, but I must point out that it takes longer and more difficult to fulfill than one might suppose. A satisfactory definition of political economy still awaits" (Walras, 1954 Ed, p.52).

Leaving aside this difficult definitional problem, one may pursue the subject by inquiring about what economics refer to as "society's problem" economics is to solve. To see how far economics as a body of scientific knowledge has come in delivering "the promised land", let us historically review the solutions offered for society's problem.

Society's Problem: Historical Development

"Since he came down from the trees man has faced the problem of survival, not as an individual, but as a member of a social group—his continued existence is testimony to the fact that he has succeeded in solving the problem, but the continued existence of wants and misery, even in the richest nations, is evidence that his solution has been at best, a partial one" (Heilbroner, 1953, p.9).

As Heilbroner puts it, man insured his survival by "organizing his society around traditions, handing down necessary tasks from one generation to the next". Adam Smith saw such a pattern in "ancient Egypt," where according to Smith, "every man was bound by principle of religion to follow the occupation of his father" (Smith, p.62). Another way the survival problem was solved was through the use of the central authoritarian rule. Thus, as Heilbroner aptly put it, "as long as the problem was handled either by tradition or by command, the economic problem never gave rise to that special field of study called economics" (Heilbroner, 1953, p.11). Hence, enters a new element for solving man's survival problem: the market system. In a market system, gain, and not tradition or authority, "steered" man to his task. The interplay of one man against another in the market insured that the tasks of society get done.

Solving man's survival problem was not the problem of prime concern to the early thinkers on the subject of economics. Indeed, the preoccupation of the writers of that period was for matters quite different. Their concern was not for the individuals survival but rather with the wealth of the nation and the wealth of a privileged few.

Two schools of thought who delved into such issues were the Mercantilists and the Physiocrats. The Mercantilists, although they did not represent a cohesive school of economic thought, nevertheless had a set of principles governing society's wealth, referred to then as social wealth.

The emergence of the Mercantilists school of thought, as Marshall put it, was a response to the prevailing philosophy, which regarded manufacturers and commerce with contempt, and was hardly "congenial to the burghers" who were proud of their handicrafts as they were of their share in governing the state. It was then that the economic theory of the Mercantilists was put forth (Marshall, 1948 Ed, p.755).

The basic tenet of the Mercantilists philosophy was that wealth consisted of gold and silver. Hence, political economy endeavored to encourage the accumulation of wealth by encouraging exports and curtailing imports. To increase the quantity of gold and silver in the country, tariffs were to be imposed on imports, and bounties (subsidies) for exports.

The Mercantilists policy of imposing high tariffs on or the prohibition of imports insured a total monopoly in the home market for domestically produced goods. The export subsidy guaranteed a flow of gold and silver to the country, thus augmenting social wealth.

Having put in place the means by which society's wealth can be increased, little attention was given to the impact of protection on the distribution of society's wealth. In effect, the monopoly granted to domestic merchants effectively increased the number of members of this class who acquired enough power not only to influence trade legislation but also other aspects of governance.

Society's problem was therefore not the survival of the individual or the allocation of society's scarce resources but rather the accumulation of gold and silver. Economics would solve this problem by devising those imposts or duties and bounties to accumulate surpluses in the balance of trade. Gold and silver was the mechanism by which surpluses (and deficits) in the balance of trade are settled.

The Mercantilists' ideas would be replaced by a school of thought that went the other way. The Physiocrats were the first to advocate free trade. This school of thought originated in France around the middle of the eighteenth century under the leadership of Quesnay. They advanced the philosophy that restriction is "artificial": that freedom is "natural". The basic principles of the doctrine were "Laissez faire, laissez passer".

The Physiocrats are viewed by many as the founders of the discipline of economics in that they developed the *Tableau*

Economique. Essentially, what the Physiocrats did was to provide a numerical accounting of society resources allocated among three classes of citizens not unlike our current National Income Accounts. The three classes are a productive class, a proprietors class, and a sterile class.

Each of these three classes has been given certain attributes. The productive class is the producer of the wealth of the nation (agriculture), the proprietary class (including the sovereign) is composed of the landowners. This class derives its revenues from the agricultural products that the producer's class generates. The third class, the sterile class consists of those citizens who are engaged in nonagricultural activities. To the Physiocrats, agriculture is the only productive resource. The sterile class or the industrial, commercial classes were viewed as unproductive. What they produced was called "immaterial" in contrast to the agricultural produce, which was called "material".

The theory did not survive the critique launched against it. The most significant criticism perhaps was its failure to provide any theory of the determination of the returns to the productive and the sterile classes, as well as the determination of the net product, which constitutes the returns to the proprietary class (Walras, 1954, p.396). As discussed later (chapter 4), the determination of the returns to factors of production fell to the English school of thought of David Ricardo and John Stuart Mill.

When, then, did society's problem become the *raison d'etre* of the science of economics? The answer is to be found in Adam Smith's *Inquiry into the Wealth of Nations*.

Although Smith equates wealth with money with gold and silver, he considered the mercantile system to be "absurd" in considering production and not consumption to be the end of industry and commerce. He further argued that "a restraint on importation of competing commodities sacrifices the interest of the consumer to the producer" (Smith, 1937 Ed, p.625).

Smith also admonished the Physiocrats for ignoring the contribution of the so-called sterile class. The "unproductive" class is not only useful, but greatly useful to the other two classes (proprietors and cultivators). "By means of the industry of merchants, artificers and manufacturers, the proprietors and cultivators, can purchase both the foreign goods and manufactures produce of their own country" (Smith, p.633).

Smith goes on to warn that any system that imposes restraints to force the allocation of society's resources toward a particular industry or activity than would otherwise be employed, is in reality "subversive of the great purpose which it means to promote. It retards instead of accelerates the progress of society toward real wealth and greatness" (Smith, p.650).

It is to be emphasized that, Smith did not espouse the interests of any particular class in society. Rather, his concern was for promoting the wealth of the entire nation. And, to Smith, wealth consisted of the goods, which all society consumes. Society's problem then was not one of allocation or distribution, but rather it concerns the creation of wealth.

As to the survival problem of the individual, Smith's solution was "nothing short of revolutionary: an astonishing game in which society assured its continuity by allowing each individual to do exactly as he saw fit as long as he followed a central game rule. The game was called the market system" (Heilbroner, 1953, p.10).

The Good, the Laborer, and the Market

Economists today have no difficulty in discussing concepts such as the "good", the "laborer" or the "Market". This was not the case however in the days of Smith, Marshall or Walras to name a few. A good place to start is with the concept of a "good".

The Good

What is a good? If a good has a "value," is that value derived from its "use" or "its exchange"? This simple concept turns out to be not simple at all as it requires, a "sustained reasoning about the use of the good" (Taussig, 1926, p.3).

A few examples illustrate the difficulties encountered in the definition of a good. Water is a good. Yet one needs to go further and define it by asking the question "is it a free good? If so, then water will have no exchange value, that is, it cannot be exchanged for money or for another good like bread. On the other hand, if water is not a free good, then one needs to ask if it commands a price or that it has a value in exchange.

The idea that a good, such as water, has a value in exchange or that it commands a price requires the establishment of ownership—whether it is a good shared by all with no "exclusion," a public good, or subject to exclusion or a private good. Defining ownership is a prerequisite for the design of an economic system. Whereas a market system is based on individual ownership of the good, a social system or a command system does not recognize private ownership, but rather a communal ownership of the good.

The question that did not arise then was that if a good was a free good, at what point will it cease to be strictly free? This question waited until the development of the field of public economics (or public finance).

These definitions of the concept of a good are at the core of the subject of economics. Moreover establishing ownership was necessary for the functioning of a market system, since in the market, value in exchange is determined. Clearly if all goods had values only in use but not in exchange, a market system would otherwise not have arisen.

The Laborer

With respect to the individual or "laborer" as was referred to, the early history of economic thought offers no specific attributes for such individual apart from being a member of the "laborer" class (Malthus, p.450), or the "sterile" class (the Physiocrats); as a supplier of his labor, a necessary input for the production of social wealth (Smith, p.8).

Malthus belittled the laborer in referring to the member of this class as "a human animal" who has no incentives to improve his lot. Since the laborer class had little in terms of material well-being, it was laid upon their shoulders their improvised condition. As Malthus put it: "The cause which has the most lasting effect in improving the situation of the lower classes of society depends chiefly upon the conduct and prudence of the individuals themselves, and is, therefore, not immediately, and necessarily connected with an increase in the means of subsistence" (p.450).

The laborer class had a champion, a defender in John Stuart Mill. First of all, he was apologetic about the use of the term "laborer class," by stating, "when I speak—of the laboring classes, or of labor as a "class," I use those phrases in compliance with customs, and as descriptive of an existing, but by no means a necessary or permanent state of social relations." Secondly, he admonished the categorization of labor as a class by stating that "there is no "class" in society which is not laboring" (Mill, 1969, p.763).

Mill, moreover, took issue with the prevailing thesis that the "labouring" class will be permanently contended with the condition of "labouring" for wages as their ultimate fortune. Arguing that as society progresses, "it is not expected that the division of the employees and employers, can be permanently maintained" (Mill, 1969, p.761).

Modern economics does not dwell on classes of individuals, the laboring classes, or landlords; rather it focuses on the characteristics of the individual as he exercises his powers over goods he consumes and the efforts (labor) he supplies. A student of economics is usually acquainted with key features of the individual that are critical for analyzing his decisions both in the goods market and the labor market.

A fundamental assumption made about the individual in modern economics is that he is "rational" (as we will see later this assumption has been challenged in the recent economic literature). By rationality, it is meant that the individual knows the alternatives before him; that he ranks these alternatives, and that if a choice is to be made, he will choose the one that "maximizes" his utility. Put differently, the individual will choose that option that yields him the highest level of satisfaction. From this it follows that if a choice before the individual involved one basket containing bread and fish and another basket containing meat and bread (both were available at the same terms), and if the individual was observed to choose the second over the first even when the first was available, then it is said that that choice offered the individual the highest level of satisfaction, hence he is rational.

Interestingly enough, whereas the foundation of modern economics was built on this proposition, the history of economic thought from the Mercantilists to Smith had little to say about "rationality". The individual was looked upon as an agent of production needed to augment social wealth, rather than a consumer of society's wealth. Whether the individual was a consumer or a producer of wealth, all such activities had to take place in the "market system".

The Market System

A simple definition would state that a market is a place where goods are exchanged. This definition is not as simple as it appears. In the old and the new economic doctrines, the existence of the market is a prerequisite for human interaction, as well as the accumulation of wealth, being all things material or immaterial, that is scarce. Three elements arise in describing a market: participants, scarcity, and gain. The phenomenon of value in exchange arises "spontaneously" in the market as a result of competition. Had all wants been satisfied with no scarcity, a market would not have existed (Walras, 1954, p.88). Had social wealth been plentiful, that is all wants satisfied with no scarcity, a market would not have existed. Moreover, if each individual through his own labor were able to satisfy his wants, there would have been no reason for exchange and no market to affect the exchange.

But social wealth by definition is all things material and immaterial that are scarce; that are both useful and available only in limited quantity. Accordingly, "scarce" things once appropriated acquire value in use and in exchange—the exchange being carried out in the market. The value acquired through the exchange is a measurable magnitude. The market then is critical not only to affect the exchange, but also to establish value.

How this value in exchange is determined clearly depends on the character of the market place and the market participants. Hence enters the tools of economics: defining ownership of the scarce good or resource and defining the market characteristics—competitive or monopolistic, regulated or free.

The student who describes the subject of economics as the study of supply and demand does not miss the mark. As long as scarcity exists, a market will exist to exchange one resource or a good for another. When each buyer and each seller finds a corresponding buyer and seller, the exchange value of the good or the resource is determined and the market for that good or the resource will be in equilibrium.

The subject of economics inquires about the characteristics of the market, the players (those who supply and those who demand the scarce resources), and the value arrived at in the exchange. This inquiry is at the essence of finding a solution to the scarcity problem.

Marshall credits Adam Smith with being the first to make a careful and scientific inquiry into the manner in which value measures human motives—on one hand measuring the desire for purchasers to obtain wealth and on the other, measuring the efforts and sacrifices undergone by its producers (Marshall, 1948 Ed, p.259).

In the marketplace the demand measures the desire (utility) for securing social wealth, the supply measures the sacrifice (disutility) associated with producing the social wealth. And, to Smith, buyer and seller left to their own devices will reap the gains from the exchange. Self-interest governs the outcome. Whether in his capacity as a buyer, a seller, or investor of his wealth, the individual will pursue the avenue that will yield him the greatest return.

Pursuing his own gain, the individual is led by an "invisible hand" to promote an end that was not part of his intention. "By pursuing his own interest he frequently promotes that of the society more effectually than when he really intends to promote it" (Smith, p.423).

The invisible hand is further strengthened in Smith's advocacy of liberal actions and against directing social wealth to specific industry or individuals toward specific activities. "That every system which endeavors, either by extraordinary encouragements to draw towards a particular species of industry a greater share of the capital of society than what would naturally go to it—is in reality subversive of the great purpose which it means to promote." Smith thus, establishes a system of "natural liberty," where every man is left perfectly free to pursue his own interest, and to bring both his industry and capital into competition with those of any man or order of man (p.65).

Mill takes issue with the principle of the invisible hand espoused by Smith. He put forth the argument that if each individual is the best judge of his own interest, this principle would prove that government ought not to exist at all.

Mill put forth an interesting argument as to why this principle is without merit by giving an example. According to Mill, "it is greatly the interest of the community collectively and individually, not to rob or defraud one another; but there is not then less necessity for laws to punish robbery and fraud, because though it is the interest of each that nobody shall rob or cheat, it is not any one's interest to refrain from rubbing and cheating others when all others are permitted to rob and cheat" (Mill, p.966).

Though elegant, this critique is a bit out of place. As will be shown in chapter 4, Smith did not rule out the role of government as a provider of security and justice for the people. Indeed as the quotation above demonstrates, the framework spelled out by Smith concerning the "invisible hand" was specific to the individual in his role as an industrialist making a decision about where to invest his capital.

Liberty, in Smith's view, demanded that the sovereign be discharged from the duty of "superintending" the industry of private people. The duty of the sovereign, then, was limited to three functions: protecting society from invasion (defense), protecting every member of society from injustice or oppression (administration of justice), and erecting and maintaining public works and public institutions that no one individual or a small number of individuals can shoulder the expense (provision of public goods). Adam Smith then not only has defined the subject of economics, but also mapped the road that society needed to travel in order to safeguard the liberty of the individual.

The subject of economics went further beyond Adam Smith's *Inquiry into the Wealth of Nations* to incorporate contributions made by David Ricardo, Alfred Marshall, John Stuart Mill, and Leon Walras. These writers developed a systematic approach to analyzing value, utility, demand, and supply, as well as problems of distribution. Their contributions established the foundations of economic analysis referred to as "principles of economics". These principles are the subject of the next chapter.

Beyond Adam Smith and the economics doctrines developed in the eighteenth and the nineteenth centuries, events have taken place in the twentieth century that necessitated a search for additional doctrines or economic principles. The Great Depression of the 1930s exposed the fragility of the discipline. New insights into the solutions to the problems facing world economies needed to be articulated in order to deal with these problems. These insights formed the body of knowledge that became known as macroeconomics. John Maynard Keynes's 1936 publication *The General Theory of Employment, Interest and Money* set the stage for the perusal of a new line of inquiry, from the goods and/or the labor market to the study of economic aggregates such as national income, employment, inflation, and economic growth.

The subject of economics was accordingly defined as consisting of two lines of inquiry: Microeconomics, and Macroeconomics. Microeconomics is where the individual and the market form the basic elements of the discipline, whereas the focus of macroeconomics is on economic aggregates such as the determination of national income, inflation, and unemployment.

Macroeconomics took center stage in the development of economics in the twentieth century. It turned Smith's world head-over-heels by insisting that the "invisible hand" is far from adequate to deal with society's problem. The "sovereign," or the government, became active and a very visible player in the economy. And once the government was recognized as an active participant, there developed a separate branch of economics, that of public finance or public economics where, the government participates actively in the affairs of the individual. Richard Musgrave, Paul Samuelson, James Buchanan, and Gordon Tullock provide the framework for such interactions.

3   ECONOMICS AS A SCIENCE

"Almost invariably the principal driving force behind the scientist's labours is the practical application of his discoveries."

—Coquelin *Traite de Credit et des Banques*

As early as the eighteenth century and especially during the nineteenth century, the body of knowledge that had been accumulated gave rise to a question that writers of the time felt the need to address. The question concerned the study of economics. A definition of the subject of economics was needed. In the search for a definition, another question was raised as to whether economics was a "science" or an "art" or whether it may be both one and the other simultaneously.

According to Coquelin, art consists of a set of precepts or rules to be followed, whereas science consists of the knowledge of certain phenomena, which have been observed or described. Put in another way, the difference between art and science lies in the fact that "art advises, prescribes and directs, whereas science observes, describes and explains" (Coquelin quoted in Walras, 1954 Ed, p.59).

Walras analyzed this proposition concluding that a distinction may have to be made between "art" and "science". Applied to political economy, there is the theory of wealth, that is the theory of exchange and value of exchange which is a science, and a theory of the production of wealth that is a theory of agriculture, industry, and trade, which is art. Hence, one may be justified in considering economics as both a science and art (Walras, pp.59-60).

Marshall in his *Principles of Economics* (Book I, chapters II through IV and in appendix B, C, and D) makes a strong case for economics being a science and for the methods and reasoning of economics. There is a great deal of overlap and repetition of the analysis and definitions presented in these two chapters and the appendices, as Marshall sought to instill in or perhaps convince his readers the idea that economics was indeed a science employing "scientific methods of inquiry".

The scientific method as defined in 1854, requires that the "principles and procedures for systematic pursuit of knowledge involving the recognition and the formulation of a problem, the collection of data through observation and experiment, and the formation and testing of hypotheses" (Merriam Webster Dictionary, p.508). Looking at the discipline of economics today, one would ascribe to it the label of science, as it clearly carries out all those functions that define the scientific method as it is used to seek solutions to economic problems.

But, at the time of the writings of Smith, Marshall, and Walras, the "science" of economics stopped short of testing the hypotheses or economics concepts that were advanced by the eighteenth and the nineteenth century as well as those before them. One can only glean the difficulties encountered by the political economists of these eras in making the case that economics is a science, as few, if any, of the economics concepts advanced had been subjected to the scientific method of inquiry. Empirical testing of propositions was not pursued until the twentieth century with the development of data and the applications of methods such as statistics from other disciplines.

The most prolific writer and defender of economics as a science involving a scientific inquiry is, without a doubt, Alfred Marshall. Yet he had a great deal of difficulty to come up with one definition that would convey the character of the discipline. To illustrate the difficulty that Marshall must have encountered in ascribing the scientific label to economics, a few quotations may be sufficient for this purpose. Marshall, in the preface to the first edition of his *Principles of Economics*, advises that "economic science is and must be one of slow and continuous growth".

Having ascribed the science label to the ideas put forth by political economists, Marshall went about to present (in his words), "a modern" of the old economic doctrines. Having espoused the notion that economics is a science, he advises his readers that economics cannot be compared with the "exact" physical sciences; for it "deals with the ever changing and subtle forces of human nature" (Marshall, 1890, 1948 Ed, p.14). Nonetheless, economics he argued differs from the branches of social sciences in that it utilizes "exact" methods of analysis.

Given that a scientific method of analyses requires not only the development of hypotheses but also testing such hypotheses, Marshall ascribes to economics the task undertaken by the other sciences of collecting facts, arranging and interpreting them as well as drawing inferences from them (p.39). Additionally, he went on to state that if economics was not a science, it aspires to be one. Economics aspires to a place among physical sciences, because "though its measurements are seldom exact—it is ever working to make them more exact".

David Ricardo, in *Principles of Political Economy and Taxation*, takes it as a *fait accompli* that economics is a science. In the preface to the third edition, he defines political economy as a "science" that is concerned with the determination of society's wealth, which he refers to as the "produce of earth" among three classes: rent, profit and wages.

Another reference to economics as a science in the writing of the political economists of the nineteenth century is found in J. B. Say "Traite d'economie politique." Marshall credits Say for placing the "science of economics in a more logical and more instructive order".

Economists today take for granted the designation of economics as a "science," a member of social sciences as it deals with the motives and decisions of individuals interacting with his fellows in society. It also deals with social issues that are in the provinces of other social sciences as well.

Unlike natural or physical sciences, economists emphasize the fact that like all "sciences," economics involves decision-making. But it differs from natural science in that unlike laboratory scientists who, according to Lord Beveridge, "never have to make decisions" (Samuelson, 1966, p.1625). Economists concerns involve decisions that are not always known in advance and are more often subject to change.

Paul Samuelson disputes the notion that laboratory scientists do not make decisions. He argued that the "problem of all sciences can be formulated as the making of intelligent decisions with respect to actual or hypothetical courses of action". He goes on to state that "a physicist or chemist need not be much of a methodologist: his discipline has a logic of its own which often will unobtrusively point the way". With softer social sciences, little "guidance" is provided by the subject matter (p.1625).

The economists' business is to be thinking about social decision-making. They exercise caution against a "loose" scientific method in that in their inquiry they dig up relevant evidence and have respect for the actual data they seek to analyze.

Samuelson sees economic problems as constantly evolving. According to Samuelson, as in all sciences, a discipline lives on its "unsolved" problem. As economics addresses society's problems, as one is resolved new ones are sure to emerge. As John Dewey said "We never step in the same river twice."

Is economics a science? If one accepts the dictionary definition of science as "the state of knowledge as distinguished from ignorance", then assuredly one can state that economics is indeed a science. In 1965, the Nobel Prize Committee issued its verdict: "Economics is a science."

4   PRINCIPLES OF ECONOMICS: THE PRIVATE ECONOMY

> "Value in Exchange, Industry and property are, then three generic phenomenon, or the three orders or graphs of specific facts which result from the limitation in quantities of utilities or the scarcity of things" (Leon Walras, *Elements of Pure Economics* (1873), 1954 Ed, p.69).

Introduction

In chapter 2, we relayed a few statements made by economists regarding the problem of society. The problem was said to be one that involves the allocation of society scarce resources, or the distribution of these resources. The definition of economics that seemed to us as "crystallizing" of what economics is about was stated by Heilbroner: "man's survival problem as a member of a social group". Unlike the novel *An Island to Oneself* by Tom Neale (1966), a man is not an island; he lives in a community, and the problem he faces is how to survive within that community.

In chapter 2 we also identified three elements that shed light on the subject of "man's survival". These are the individual, the goods, and the market. In this chapter, we address the principles that govern the activities of the individual as he interacts with his fellow individuals in society. In such interactions, he is either a seller of his own goods, a buyer of someone else's goods, or both. These interactions takes place in a setting called the market or the private economy.

Political economists of the eighteenth and nineteenth centuries, beginning with Adam Smith, have dealt with individuals interactions in an organized setting—a market—where goods and services are exchanged. Although Smith, along with other eighteenth—and nineteenth-century political economists, recognized the presence of another player in the national economy: the government, the "visible" hand of government did not intrude sufficiently into the analysis or the principles derived.

Since our focus in this chapter is on the principles that govern the individual behavior in the market place, we shall abstract from the analysis the role played by the government in the economy, in terms of its impact on market characteristics as well as on the individual activities as a consumer or a producer of private goods.

In modern economic thought, the point of departure in analyzing individual behavior in the market place is to identify characteristics specific to the individual that explain his behavior in the market place. The most significant characteristic is "rationality". To be rational, the individual in the market place is assumed to know all the alternatives before him, that he ranks these alternatives, and if a choice is to be made he chooses the option that gives him the highest level of satisfaction (that is he maximizes his utility). As we shall see later, the assumption of rationality has come under a great deal of scrutiny.

Historically, this was not always the case. The individual characteristics did not come up in the analysis of market exchange. To analyze such an exchange, the "goods" coming to the market had to be described the production process and the factors of production identified. Market characteristics, whether competitive or subject to monopoly influence, were also addressed. The source of goods coming to the market, whether domestically produced or imported, although dealt with in the analysis, the coverage of the subject was limited to the effects of such activities, imports and exports on the balance of trade, and on tax policy.

Smith, Marshall, Ricardo, Mill, and Walras provide an extensive analysis—descriptive as well as analytical—of the production and exchange of goods. Concepts such as "value," "exchange," "rent," "wages," and "profits", all economics concepts were defined, and their determination explained. Inspection of the table of contents of these writers' volumes reveals the thought process that went into the formation of a theory of prices of final products, "market goods", hence the determination of the "exchange" values of the goods (the consumption side of the economy). Moreover, one can discern how a theory of factor returns is derived from the interplay of market forces (the production side of the economy).

Smith, Mill, and Marshall began their inquiry by focusing on the production side of the economy. Ricardo and Walras approached the subject of economics by focusing on the determination of values of goods in exchange, hence establishing a theory of market exchanges. Analyses of the production side, particularly the determination of factors remuneration were not ignored, but followed the analysis of the goods market.

By far the most extensive analysis of the goods market is provided by Marshall where he devoted fifteen chapters of the book to the subject in order to establish an economic framework (demand and supply) for the determination of value. Walras, although more "frugal" in his exposition, is more formidable in his analysis of the goods market, especially for his introduction of the logic of scientific inquiry, the use of mathematics to derive the exchange value of market goods.

Modern textbooks at the introductory level are not uniform in their approach to the historical exposition of the subject. Paul Samuelson's introductory text, *Economics* (1948), followed the practices of Smith, Mill, and Marshall by focusing first on the production side of the economy, relegating the consumption side to a secondary place (part three of his volume, 1948).

Of interest is the fact that introductory textbooks in economics in the twentieth century, notably Samuelson and few of his contemporaries have devoted a great deal of attention to an analysis of the macro economy—the determination of national income and its fluctuations, rather than the micro side of the economy. This practice was prompted in part by the emphasis placed on the behavior of the aggregate magnitudes, an area of economic study that took hold following the publication of Keynes's *The General Theory of Employment, Interest and Money* in 1936.

At the advanced levels of study, the current practice is to divide the body of economic knowledge into two areas: microeconomics and macroeconomics. Whereas macroeconomics deals with the determination of national output (national income), employment, inflation, and interest (aggregate magnitudes), microeconomics deals with determinants of the consumption and production sides of the economy—a subject that occupied the political economists of the eighteenth and nineteenth centuries.

Keeping in mind that the study of the macro economy is a twentieth century phenomenon, our journey into the development of economic thought during the eighteenth and nineteenth centuries will focus on the "micro" aspect of the subject of economics. The Keynesian perspective on economics (macroeconomics) will be dealt with in chapter 5 in the volume.

Recall that at the beginning of the chapter we highlighted man's "survival problem" as one involving his interaction with his fellow citizens in society. The place to start, then, in the historical review is with the exchange that takes place in the market. To do so, we need to identify the elements that have to exist for an exchange to take place. This involves the determination of value, the goods, and services to be exchanged, as well as the character of the market itself.

The Market: Determinants of Value in Exchange

For goods to have values, they will either have value in use, exchange, or both. If a good cannot meet any of these standards it ceases to be an economic good—a "good" that commands value. A good that only has a value in use, but not in exchange, will have value only to its users. Therefore it cannot be exchangeable for other goods. In other words, it has no market value. Hence, for a market to exist there has to be goods that command values in exchange.

The players in the market are of two types: those who possess the goods and those who wish to acquire the goods. The interaction in the market between those who are in possession of the goods and those who seek to acquire them set the exchange values of the goods.

Economic analysis deals with goods that have exchange values, which by definition must have use values, the exception being collective goods that are provided by the governments free of charge and are thus not subject to the exchange. Worth noting is the fact that the exchange outcome not only sets the price of the goods transacted but also acts as a clearing mechanism for the exchange.

We have mentioned above, that Adam Smith and Alfred Marshall began their treatises on the principles of economics with an analysis of the production side of the economy—especially the determination of the returns to the factors of production; wages, rent, profits, and interest. The logic behind the analysis of production prior to that of consumption may be considered as a prerequisite to the analysis of value in exchange, for whatever goods are brought to the market for exchange, a value had to be arrived at somehow. If the exchange involves a "stock", such as gold, land, houses, and the like, their value is determined in the market by exchanging one stock for another. If the exchange involves a "flow," such as labor services and/or land services, then one needs to establish values for these flows. As will be discussed below, the production side of the economy establishes values for both stocks and flows.

For a laborer to participate in an exchange in the goods market, he must first participate in the production economy exchanging his labor services for gold or another form of currency. Once that has been accomplished, the laborer is able to acquire the desired goods in the goods market.

Similarly, the owners of the other factors of production, such as the landlords, they too have to bring their land into production and using the rent obtained from placing the land in production to become a participant in the goods market. Determination of factors returns such as wages; returns to labor, rents; returns to land, and profits; returns on capital, precedes the participation of the individual in the goods market. Accordingly, to understand what has been referred to as man's survival problem; we must begin with the man in his role either as a laborer, landowner, or a capitalist.

Political economists of the eighteenth and nineteenth centuries offer a comprehensive analysis of exchanges in the goods and factors markets and consequently the determination of the exchange values in the market place. Smith, Ricardo, Marshall, and Walras offer analyses of the goods and the factors-of-production markets deriving, the equilibrium conditions in these markets. As we seek to review the foundations upon which modern microeconomic theory was built, we shall offer a chronological review of the economic principles governing the exchange.

It is worth emphasizing from the outset that our historical review will undoubtedly be incomplete, not only because of the dimensions of the subject, but also because of the overlap in coverage and methods of analysis employed by the political economists of the eighteenth and nineteenth centuries. It also reflects the limitations we have imposed on ourselves in selecting the contributions of only few eighteenth—and nineteenth-century economists to use as the basis of the analyses of the subject of economics and the role of the economist.

Walras posits a chicken-and-egg question, the answer to which would provide guidance as to the sequence of analysis of the private economy; that is whether one ought to begin with the consumption economy or the production economy. Walras pondered the following question: "Whether the price of productive services determines the prices of products, or whether the prices of products having been already determined—by the operation of the law of offer and demand, determines, in their turn the prices of the productive services by the operation of the law of cost of production or cost price" (Walras, p.212).

If one were to examine the textbooks of economics that we currently use in introductory courses in economics, one would find neither Walras's question posed, nor the answer to that query given. The explanation lies in the way the subject of economics at the introductory level is introduced.

Microeconomic analysis would either begin with supply and demand in the goods market or supply and demand of factor services in the factors market, and thus the determination of goods prices in the goods market and the returns to factors in the factors market. The link between the two markets, the price/cost determination is seldom made at this juncture, because to do so requires a general equilibrium framework for the simultaneous determination of all prices and quantities. Walras provided that framework (*Elements*, lessons 18,

19, and 20). Unfortunately his analyses of general equilibrium did not make it in the introductory textbooks in economics.

Our historical review of the principles put forth for the operation of private markets for goods and factor services begins with Adam Smith's *Inquiry into the Wealth of Nations*.

Adam Smith on the Division of Labor and Society's Wealth

The question posited by Walras relayed above was where Smith analysis of the "division of labour" takes us. Smith began by setting forth principles that govern the division of labor. One may ask: why start there? The answer is simple: Smith's *Inquiry into the Wealth of Nations* is about the sources of the "Wealth of Nations". The point of departure, then, is an inquiry into these sources.

To Smith, "labour is the real measure of exchangeable value of all other commodities" (p.30). From this proposition, it follows that the exchanges where values for goods and services are determined start with labor services.

According to Smith, labor was the first price, the original purchase money that was paid for all things. It was not gold or silver, but by labor, that all the wealth of the world was originally purchased; and its value, to those who possess it, and who wants to exchange it for some new production, is precisely equal to the quantity of labour which it can enable them to purchase or demand.

On close inspection, one arrives at the answer to the riddle put forth by Walras. The exchange is the equilibrating mechanism where labor services and goods values are determined simultaneously. Labor services, then, is the money measured by the quantity supplied, which in turn determines the quantity bought of market goods and hence their prices. From this exposition we have:

The first principle of Microeconomics:

Labor services determine the exchange values of all goods.

Labor (at the time) was viewed as the only source of wealth; accordingly Smith directed his inquiry toward identifying those elements that would increase wealth. Smith found the answer in the division of labor.

Accordingly, Smith went about extolling the benefits of this principle by enumerating the beneficial effects of the division of labor in business, because as he put it: "the nature of agriculture does not admit of so many subdivisions of labour". The principles that give rise to the division of labor may be stated as follows:

- The division of labor is limited by the extent of the market.
- In the division of labor, once established, every man lives by exchanging labor for goods.
- Difficulties in bartering (such as labor services for other services) give rise to another commodity: money.

Having established the necessity for the use of a mechanism of exchange beside labor (money), he turned to the determination of the prices (exchange values) of the commodities. This approach is what is referred to in modern economics as "partial equilibrium" analyses.

Exchange Value

Following the establishment of the initial source of national wealth and the way to enhance such wealth, Smith turned to the question of the determination of the exchange value of goods. As a starting point he put forth the proposition that the value of any commodity is set by the quantity of labor. But labor is not of one kind (homogeneous). It varies; hence it is difficult to ascertain the exchangeable values of commodities if it was not easy to ascertain the proportion between different quantities of labor. This then meant that exchangeable value has to be set in term of the quantity of some other commodity. Moreover, Smith pointed out that often one commodity is exchanged for other commodities; therefore its value may be determined by something other than the quantity of labor, namely money.

The concept that value in exchange has to be expressed in money led to the development of a theory of value. Three questions were addressed: First, what is the real measure of the exchangeable value? Second, what are the different components of this real price? And third, under what conditions the market price is likely to diverge from the real price? To answer these questions, Smith developed the concepts of "nominal" price, and the real price of commodities. The real price is measured by the quantity of labor; the nominal price by the quantity of money paid for the commodity.

This exposition sets the principles governing the exchangeable value of commodities as given below:

- The real measure of the exchangeable value of all commodities is "labor".
- Labor services are not uniform; the exchangeable value of two commodities with different quantities of labor may be difficult to measure.
- The real price and nominal price of all commodities are exactly in proportion to one another at the same time and place.

What about Labor?

Like commodities, labor may be said to have a real price and a nominal price. The real price is measured by the "quantities of necessaries" and "conveniences of life" which are given for it; the nominal price is the quantity of money paid for labor services.

Next, Smith made the transition from exchange value to price.

From Exchange Value to Price

To derive a theory of value and price, Smith meshes the two sides of the market: the production and the consumption sides of the economy.

As stated earlier, labor services, according to Smith, is the real measure of value. But, labor services originate in the production side of the economy; labor is employed in conjunction with other factors of production either in agriculture or industry. In the production economy labor adds value to the materials (other inputs) used in production. According to Smith, when "stock" (capital) has been accumulated and used, the value labor add to the materials will resolve itself in this case into two parts, of which the one pays their wages, the other the profits (Smith, p.48). Similarly, if land is used along with labor, then the value the worker adds is divided: rent to the landlord and wages for the workman.

Having linked the two sides of the economy, Smith then proceeded to explain how commodity prices and the price of factor services are determined. To do so he advanced two concepts: the "natural" price and the "market" price. The natural price of a commodity is that which is sufficient to pay for the services of the factors of production. That is, the price is sufficient to cover the wage paid to labor, the profit to the owner of the stock, and the rent to the landlord. These values are "set by the circumstances of society—their riches or poverty, their advancey, stationary or declining condition; and partly by the particular nature of each employment" (Smith, p.55). In modern terminology, Smith's natural price may be said to correspond to an equilibrium price or a stationary state price.

The market price is the outcome of the interplay of supply and demand. Hence, the price of a commodity may be higher or lower than the natural price. From this analysis, a market price may be stated as follows: The market price exactly equates the value of the commodity with the returns to factors of production.

Having dispensed with the determination of value in exchange, Smith devoted the bulk of his *Inquiry into the Wealth of Nations* to the determination of the returns to factors—wages, rent, and profits. We shall return to this exposition in a later section of the chapter.

The next classical economist to address society's problem was Robert Malthus, who wrote two volumes on the topic; one deals mostly with population, while the other deals with principles of economics. His essay on population is one that had attracted a great deal of attention, hence his view expressed here are based on his thesis on population.

Robert Malthus on Value

Malthus took a different approach to that of Smith to solving society's problem. In his population volume he did not discuss the determination of value rather, he addressed society's problem, as one of imbalance between two natural forces: population growth and the growth of food or subsistence. Malthus offered a prospect that was meager, dreary, and shilling. This bleak picture appeared first in an anonymous treatise consisting of 50,000 words with the title, "An Essay of Population as it Affects the Future Improvement of Society" (1798). This theme was carried out and expanded in his volume on population.

To place Malthus's contribution to the study of the private economy, one needs to sort out two streams of thought embodied in his analyses: one focuses exclusively on the "poor", the "poor laboring class" and the second focuses on the imbalance between two natural forces—population growth and the growth of food or subsistence.

In the introduction to his volume, Malthus stated a fundamental proposition that underlay his preoccupation with the population question: "To restore a sense of the predictable as opposed to the ideal." He saw society's problem as a "deep-seated evil" in the principle of population. Simply put, that "the power of population (propagation) is infinitely greater than the power of earth to produce subsistence for man". From this he deduced two principles:

- That food and sexual passions are both essential to human existence and, secondly,
- That while food increases only in "arithmetical ratio, population when unchecked increases in geometrical ratio" (p.157).

This deduction led him to postulate two other principles:
- Population is limited by the means of subsistence.
- Population invariably increases when the means of subsistence increases, unless it was subject to checks.

The checks that would keep the population on a level with the means of subsistence are moral restraint, vice, and misery.

Malthus's focus on population growth in relation to subsistence can be put down as a focus on the supply or the production side of the economy. Unlike Smith, Ricardo, Marshall, and other eighteenth and nineteenth-century political economists, Malthus's preoccupation with the relative reproductive capacity of two factors, labor and land, has succeeded in shifting the public focus away from Smith's innovative approach to enhancing the nation's wealth through the division of labor to the unharmonious universe where the propagation of human being outstrips the propagation of food stuffs.

As Malthus's exposition in the population volume deals mainly with the implications of the principles of population, the conditions that affect the laboring classes, as well as those that affect subsistence, laborers' wages, and landlords' rent, the proper place for putting down his postulates is in the section of the chapter dealing with the determination of returns to factors of production.

We turn next to the contributions of David Ricardo, John Stuart Mill, Leon Walras, and Alfred Marshall to the theory of value.

David Ricardo on the Theory of Value

Unlike Adam Smith, Ricardo began his treatises with the study of value. In the preface to his volume, he remarked: "I have endeavored to explain more fully, my opinion on the difficult subject of value Indeed Ricardo painstakingly thought to come up with a clear, although not concise, definition of the concept and in doing so challenged some of the statements about value put forth earlier by Adam Smith in his "Inquiry".

As previously mentioned, Smith attributed the value of a commodity to the relative quantity of labor used in its production. Ricardo, on the other hand injects value in use or utility as a necessary requirement to establish value. Having possessed this feature, he argued, that the value in exchange for a commodity depends on two sources: scarcity and the quantity of labor required to produce it.

Ricardo modified this proposition somewhat by arguing that there are commodities, the value of which is determined by their scarcity alone. No amount of labor can increase the quantity of such goods, and therefore their value in exchange cannot be lowered or increased by an increase in supply (e.g. rare books and art).

Although scarcity is one of the sources of exchangeable value, nonetheless Ricardo agrees with Smith that for the greatest part of commodities, the exchangeable value depends almost exclusively on the quantity of labor expended on them. This modification then reinforces Smith's principle that the value in exchange depends on the quantity of labor.

A more fundamental critique was leveled by Ricardo against some of Smith's other propositions, which tie in the exchangeable values of commodities to the proportion of labor employed in their production and/or the reward of labor. According to Ricardo, "if a man's labour had become doubly efficient, and he could therefore produce twice the quantity of a commodity, he would necessarily receive twice the former quantity in exchange for it." Having put this proposition forward, he proceeded to question its validity. "If the proposition was valid, then "the reward of the labour were always in proportion to what he produced, the quantity of labour bestowed on a commodity and the quantity of labour which that commodity would purchase would be equal and either might accurately measure the valuation of things." Clearly this is not the case, as labor is not an "invariable" standard of value.

Ricardo went on to discuss criteria that have to be met for a commodity, such as corn or labor (both examples were used by Smith) to be an invariable standard of value. He dismisses both, arguing that this standard is not met by any commodity, including gold and silver.

According to Ricardo, when Smith uses labor as a standard, he speaks not of the quantity of labor bestowed on the product of any object, but the quantity which it can command in the market as if the two are equivalent.

Ricardo questions this proposition by stating that the value of labor is "equally variable," as it is affected by the proportion between the supply and demand, prices of goods on which wages are spent, and so on. Having put forth what he thought as shortcomings of Smith's exposition of the determination of exchangeable value of commodities, he expounded on the concept by introducing new elements into the analysis. These new elements have in modern literature become very critical in the analyses of market demand and supply and the determination of prices. These elements are the use of capital, fixed and circular, in the production process; the comparative skill and intensity of labor required in the production of goods; and the time required to bring the goods to market. All these elements describe the dynamics of the production process, which have a bearing on the value of a commodity over time.

Ricardo's contribution to the discussion of value is his postulate that both capital (the ratio of fixed to circular) of different durability, as well as labor of different qualities and intensity, figure prominently in determining exchangeable value of commodities. What Ricardo outlined at that time is now described as "embodied technology" in the factor of production, which clearly governs not only its use but also its contribution to the final product.

The principles one drives from Ricardo's superb exposition of the dynamics of production, and hence the exchangeable value of commodities, may be stated as follows:

- The exchangeable value of a commodity would be in proportion to the labour used in their production, not on their immediate production only, but would include all those factors such as machinery embodied in labor.
- The quantity of labor used in the production of commodities in conjunction with the use of capital fixed and circular regulates the relative value of commodities.
- The degree to which an alteration in the relative value of goods (rise or fall) will depend on the proportion of fixed capital to total capital use in production of the good.

Clearly, Ricardo has set the stage for the integration of the production side of the economy with the measurements of value in the market place. As demonstrated above, he introduced dynamic elements to the determination of value, in particular, the embodied capital in labor services, capital durability and the capital labor ratio. According to Ricardo: these elements "constitute the real foundation of exchange value" (Ricardo, 1952 Ed, p.25). We turn next to the exposition of John Stuart Mill.

John Stuart Mill on Value

Unlike his fellow political economists of the eighteenth and nineteenth centuries, Mill was much more concerned with moral and philosophical issues than Smith (in the *Wealth of Nations*), Ricardo, or Marshall. He devoted little time (15 pages out of 1,000) to the analysis of value.

Like Adam Smith, his predecessor, he began his analysis by identifying elements that give rise to value. However, he made it clear that his views of what constitute value differ from Smith's as well as from the definitions supplied by other political economists in that, in his view, they did not make a distinction between the price of a thing (a commodity) from its value. According to Mill: "The word value, when used without adjunct, always means in political economy, value in exchange; or as it has been called by Adam Smith and his successors, exchangeable value, a phrase which no amount of authority that can be quoted for it can make other than bad English" (Mill, 1969 Ed, p.437).

To Mill, value in exchange should not be confused with price. Whereas price expresses the value of a "thing" in term of money, the exchange value of a thing is the general power of purchasing or the "command" over things in general. The distinction between the value in exchange and the price was described by the following:

- All things (commodities) may experience rise in their money prices, but there cannot be a general rise in values.
- Things that are exchanged for one another can no more all fall or rise together.
- For a thing to have value in exchange, it must be of some use (utility), and there must be some difficulties in its attainment (p.442).

The third postulate does not differ much from that which was offered by Smith. What Mill sought was needed to be highlighted is perhaps an emphasis on the determination of value in exchange vis-à-vis the price.

Mill enumerated those factors that would give rise to the value in exchange; limited supply or scarcity, articles that are "necessaries" of life, and/or articles that are in nature limited in supply. But for the majority of things, value depends on market forces of supply and demand.

It is worth noting that Mill made a distinction between what he referred to as a "temporary" market value and "natural" value. He stated the difference in the following:

- The temporary market value of a thing depends on the demand and supply.
- The natural value is a scarcity value, which depends on the temporary value but also on the cost of production.

Whether the value is temporary or natural, the essence of Mill's argument is that value and price (although he made the distinction), depend on both sides of the market; demand and supply.

Leon Walras on Value

Walras put forth his own views with respect to the "origin" of value. According to Walras, there are three major approaches to the solution of value: the first is that of Adam Smith and David Ricardo, which he termed the English solution. This solution, traces the origin of value to "labor." The second solution is the "French" solution advanced by J. B. Say, which traces the origin of value to utility; the third solution is that of A. A. Walras (the father of Leon Walras also a political economist), which traces the origins of value to scarcity. According to Leon Walras this is the correct solution, that is, value is derived from scarcity.

Walras took issue with Smith's assertion that all things that have value and are exchangeable are labor in one form or another, so that labor alone constitutes the whole of social wealth. This critique is in line with Ricardo's notion that not all values are labor values. Like Ricardo, Walras pointed out that certain things (like rare art or wine) not derived from labor which have value are exchangeable and constitute wealth (Walras, 1954 Ed, p.261). Hence, he argued, whether labor is all or part of social wealth is beside the point; in either case the proper questions to ask are: First, is labor worth anything? And secondly, why is it exchangeable? According to Walras, Smith failed to address these two questions.

Additional criticism was launched by Walras against both Ricardo's and Mill's categorization of commodities: those whose quantities are augmented by labor and those commodities that could not be expanded by an increase in the quantity of labor. Walras reproduced the exact statements appearing in both Ricardo and Mill (see above) regarding these two classifications of commodities. He then proceeded to point out two errors in their positions.

The first error concerned the notion espoused by both Ricardo and Mill, that the first type of commodities can be "multiplied without limit" and that a certain value of their cost determines their selling price. The source of error, according to Walras, arises from the fact that there are "no products that can be multiplied without limit; land, labour and capital services exist only in limited quantities". The second error, according to Walras, arises from Ricardo and Mill notions that the value of commodities being determined by the cost of production. According to Walras, there exists no "one value" for the cost of production, which having itself been determined, determines in turn the selling prices of products. The selling price of products is determined in the market by two elements; their utility and their quantity (Walras, p.402).

Walras addressed his own questions posed earlier as to whether labor constitutes social wealth; whether labor has value, and whether labor has exchangeable value. He answered these questions by positing that if labor has value and is exchangeable, it is because it is both useful and limited in quantity; that is, it is scarce. Value then is derived from scarcity, and "utility" makes it desirable. Walras then emphasized the fact that utility alone is not enough for goods to command a price (to have exchangeable value), their scarcity matters most.

Walras next engaged into a lengthy dialogue as to why exchangeable value (price) depends on these two elements. To Walras, "these two elements are the true foundations of the price of things".

To solve for the exchangeable value or the price of commodities, he presented first, a theory of "simultaneous" determination of the prices of products and the prices of factors of production (land, services, personal services, and capital services); and second, he presented a theory of the determination of the rate of net income and corresponding prices of all types of capital used in production; and third, he presented a theory of the determination of all prices in terms of money. Walras analyses are "general equilibrium" analyses, where all prices are determined simultaneously through the interplay of supply and demand in all markets. By its nature the framework is cast in terms of simultaneous equations, which in some respect obscured its value for advancing a significant theory of value.

Putting aside the mathematical framework and the simultaneous equations used for the derivation of all prices, Walras's contribution to the theory of value can be expressed by the following principles:

- Utility and scarcity are the two necessary elements for the determination of exchangeable value.
- Labor has a value and exchangeable because it is both useful and limited in quantity.
- Value comes from scarcity; utility makes it desirable.
- Value in exchange is a magnitude that is measurable using a unit of measurement.
- Value in exchange is a property which certain goods possess and that can be bought and sold.
- The value in exchange manifests itself in the marketplace.

Alfred Marshall on Value

Marshall's *Principles of Economics* by all accounts is considered a landmark in the science of economics. Unlike Ricardo and Walras, Marshall neither dwelled on definitions of concepts, nor took issue with some of Smith's or Ricardo's exposition of their theories of value. Rather, he set about formulating principles of economics that govern the market determination of demand and supply and the price of commodities.

In the preface to his volume, Marshall states: "The present treatise is an attempt to present a modern version of old doctrines with the aid of the new work, and with reference to the new problems, of our age."

In Book II, chapter I, Marshall introduces the main theme that has occupied many political economists of the nineteenth century—that of wants and their satisfaction. This in essence epitomizes the search for a solution of man's survival problem. Had resources been plentiful, the issue would not have arisen. But, resources are scarce and man's wants are forever increased. This then sets the departure point in Marshall's formulation of the "Principles of Political Economy".

Marshall began by building a structure to analyze the production side of the economy (Book II), which was followed by a "Theory of Demand and Supply" which occupies Book V, chapters 1-15. He concluded his treatise by analyzing issues relating to the distribution of national income.

Marshall's arrangement of topics is in line with Smith's own, in focusing first on the wealth of a nation and then on the production process, prior to addressing the question he had raised in the preface about "wants" and their satisfaction. Below are Marshall's analyses of these three elements.

Wealth, Wants, and Distribution

In chapter I, Book II, Marshall began by defining the concept of wealth: "Wealth consists of desirable things which satisfy human wants; directly or indirectly; but not all desirable things are reckoned as wealth" (p.54). Desirable things may either be material or immaterial. Material things consist of things that yield benefits to the owner, whereas immaterial things are those embodied in man's qualities and/or external relations useful to the individual.

Marshall then enhanced the definition of wealth to include immeasurable magnitudes that may or may not have value in exchange, although they might impact labor's contribution to the production of goods. However, Marshall, having advanced this broader view of wealth, he dismissed it in his analysis of market exchanges, since exchangeable value, according to Marshall is determined not by the individual possession of "personal wealth"—immaterial goods, but by "material wealth".

Next, Marshall turned to the question of wants and their satisfaction. Of interest is the way Marshall affected a transition in the analysis from the concepts of wants and demand to show why a theory of demand or exchange must follow the analysis of production and the supply of efforts.

In his Principles, Marshall states: "Human wants and desires are countless in number and very various in kind" (p.86). In the early stages of man's existence, these wants give rise to activities (labor supply), to satisfy these wants. Afterward, new activities give rise to new wants. Thus, the theory of wants and their satisfaction (demand and consumption), must follow a theory of efforts (supply of labor).

To build a theory of demand, Marshall needed to link wants and desires to the concept of utility, and from that to price. Given that wants and desires cannot be measured directly, if utility is taken to be "the outward" phenomenon to which they give rise, the price is what a person is willing to pay for the satisfaction of his desire.

There is an endless variety of wants, but there is a limit to each separate want (this is the concept of satiation). This fundamental tendency of human nature is stated as the law of diminishing utility. From the concept of satiation, Marshall's analysis may be expressed by the following principles governing wants and their satisfaction:

- Total utility of a thing (good) to the individual increases with every increase of his stock of it.
- The additional benefit derived from an increase in the stock of things diminishes with every increase in the stock the individual already has; everything else remains the same.
- An increase in the stock of a thing at a "uniform" rate, the benefit derived from it increases at a "diminishing" rate (diminishing marginal utility principle).

Translating these principles in terms of goods prices the following principles may be stated:
- Marginal demand price is that which equates the utility at the margin that is the utility of the last unit.
- Demand is said to be efficient when the price the individual is willing to offer is equal to the price others are willing to pay.
- A complete knowledge of the demand for a good requires knowledge of the quantity the individual is willing to purchase at each of the prices it is likely to be offered for (the demand schedule).

Marshall next made the transition from the individual demand to the market demand as follows:

Under the assumption that the demand of a single individual is fairly representative of the general demand for a whole market (this assumption about the individual has become known in the modern literature as the representative individual), the general law of demand can be stated:

- The greater the quantity to be sold, the smaller must be the price at which it is offered. In other words, the amount demanded increases as the price falls, and diminishes as the price rises (this gives a downward slopping demand schedule).
- The price measures the marginal utility of the good to each buyer.
- The price paid for a good is not a measure of marginal utility in "general," because wants and circumstances of individuals are different.

Next Marshall tied in the rate of change of utilities of goods to the stock (amount) the individual possess of the good by offering the concept of the "elasticity" of wants. According to Marshall, the rate of decline in desire, or utility, of a good diminishes, everything being equal, with every increase in the supply (the diminishing marginal utility principle). However, the decline is not constant; it may be slow or rapid, depending on the elasticity of demand. Hence:

- The demand is said to be elastic, if the fall in the quantity demanded is large for a small rise in price and vice versa.
- What holds for the individual demand (elasticity), holds for the market (aggregate) demand. That is, if the individual demand is elastic, the total demand will also be elastic.
- Exceptions from the general principles apply: low elasticity for "necessaries," high elasticity for "luxuries".
- Markets for goods may be perfect or imperfect. Perfect markets are characterized by many buyers and sellers; imperfect markets are characterized by few buyers and sellers.

The next stage in the analyses was the introduction of a unit of exchange; money. To introduce money in the exchange process, Marshall stresses the point that "barter" may be the way goods can be exchanged in the market. However, this method can only be feasible where few goods are subject to exchange and/or where only a small and limited amount of goods are subject to exchange. "Difficulty in barter" is small when there are a few simple commodities, but when there are numerous goods and numerous buyers and sellers, there is urgent need for the use of a general purchasing power—money.

Marshall using the concept advanced earlier, value and utility to derive the "consumer surplus". To arrive at this concept, Marshall ponders the question of whether the price an individual actually pays for a thing represents the benefit (the utility) that the individual derives from its possession. Having pointed out that this subject had received little attention from his predecessors, he formulated the concept of consumers' surplus by pointing out that the price a person pays for a thing can never exceed and seldom corresponds to that which he would be willing to pay, rather than going without the thing. In other words, the satisfaction he receives exceeds what he has given up in paying the price. The difference is the "consumer surplus". Thus we may state Marshall's ideas by the following principles:

- The real worth of things to the individual is not measured by the price he pays for them.
- Utility of income declines as income rises; "a pound worth of satisfaction to a poor man is greater than a pound's worth of satisfaction to a rich man".

Having established these principles, Marshall offered in Book V an analysis of supply and demand and the determination of prices, and consumer surplus.

The next stage in the analysis is to formulate a theory of market supply and from it to derive the returns to factors of production. Again we begin with Smith's exposition.

Market Supply and the Returns to Factors

As relayed above, Marshall emphasized the notion that in a barter economy one needs to barter something for something else. Hence, for a laborer to satisfy his wants or desires, he needs to offer something (his labor services) to acquire it. This, accordingly, sets the stage for the development of the supply side of the market, where services are traded for goods (in a barter economy) or for money in a market economy where money circulates.

The analysis of the supply side of the market is a bit more complex than the demand side, as there are multiple factors of production that are used for producing a supply of goods. Moreover, not all goods are produced by the same factor combinations. Accordingly, one needs to focus on the production process and or factors combinations as well as the returns to factors.

Adam Smith

Beginning with Adam Smith (Book II), we find the subject to be well expressed in the following observation: "In a society in which there is no division of labour, in which exchanges are seldom made, and in which every man provides everything for himself, it is not necessary that any stock should be accumulated" (Smith, p.259).

The essence of production and supply, then, is the accumulation of stock, which can only take place under the principle of the division of labor. In other words, the division of labor makes it necessary for the accumulation of stock and hence production and supply.

Having established the principle of the division of labor as fundamental to the production process, Smith turned his attention to the definition of the "stock". Two subdivisions of stock have to be distinguished: circulating capital and fixed capital. Labor, too, was subdivided into two categories: productive and unproductive. After defining the factors of production, capital (stock), and labor and their subdivision, Smith proceeded next to build a theory of factor remunerations in the production economy beginning with labor. From his analyses we can derive the following principle:

- The produce of labor determines labor's compensation when neither land nor stock (capital) is employed along with labor in production.

Given that the production process requires the employment of other factors, like stock and land; Smith addressed the implication of the use of these factors for the returns of labor.

Several things are at play: land is used to produce "subsistence" stock and materials with which labor services are added. Hence the "product" of labor no longer belongs to labor alone, it has to be divided among these three factors.

Next, Smith introduces a new player in the production process, a "master," which in modern economic terminology is referred to as the "entrepreneur" (see also Walras reference to the entrepreneur below). The master's job is to direct labor to perform their tasks (presumably more efficiently), and with this addition the product of labor will have to cover, in addition, the services of the master. What the "master" received is a negotiable amount between labor and the master (a precursor to the contract theory).

It is worth noting that Smith's analysis of the production side of the economy did not focus on the derivation of the supply of commodities or on the derivation of their cost. Rather, his focus was on the determination of factor returns, wages, rent, and profits and from the returns to factors to the demand and the supply of these factors. Hence, Smith derived both the demand and supply from the remuneration of labor.

According to Smith, the demand for labor is governed by a "wage fund". He distinguished two types of funds: a "revenue fund" where there would be an amount of revenues that would exceed the wages paid to workers; there, Smith uncouples labor's contribution to production of goods (their products) from what the labor is paid from the wage fund. What the labor is paid is what Smith called the amount that covers the maintenance of the worker. The second is the stock fund, which is over and above what is needed in the production process. Accordingly, the demand for labor cannot rise until the wage fund increases. The price of labor then depends on two things: the demand for labor, which depends on the wage fund, and the price of necessaries and convenience of life. This then ties in the money price of labor services to the price of necessaries (subsistence). From these propositions, the demand for labor is established:

- The demand for labor, whether rising, falling, or stationary determines the quantities of necessaries obtained by labor.
- The money price of labor is higher when the price of the necessaries is lower.
- The money price of labor depends on what is required to produce the necessaries of life.
- The increase in the wage increases the price of many commodities.

As an afterthought to the determination of wages, Smith points out that the wage the laborer received depends on the hardship or ease of employment and the condition of work. Again this has become an important element in the determination of labor supply in modern economic theory and is referred to as the disutility of work.

From the above presentation of Smith's thesis, it is difficult to come to grips with what determines the wage or the returns to labor services. The question that needs to be asked is whether or not the basket of goods the laborer consumes determines labor's returns. In our modern terminology, this is the basket of goods that make up the cost of living index. If this were so, the question then is: under what condition does the product of labor exceed that level? And if so, to whom does the surplus value accrue?

If as Smith maintained, this increases the surplus in the wage fund, would that increase necessarily give rise to an increase in the demand for labor, irrespective of the market demand for goods produced by the employment of labor?

As we go through the contributions of Ricardo, Mill, Walras, and Marshall, these questions as well as others, will be addressed. Also, wage determination in conjunction with the demand and supply of labor will be clarified.

The next question addressed by Smith is whether profits and rent constitute the returns to capital (the stock) and land. Smith offered key factors that figure prominently in the determination of profit: the economic condition and the market characteristics. From his analysis we can deduce the following:

- The ordinary rate of profit in all types of employment of capital in the production of goods varies with the certainty or uncertainty of the return to capital.
- The rate of return to capital depends on the size of the market.
- Restraining competition adversely affects both the rate of profit and the wage rate.
- The proportion between the rates of wages and profits is invariant to the state of the economy, whether it is advancing, declining, or stationary.

Of interest is Smith's digression at this point to offer a remark that has been neglected often in discussing the libertarian, laissez-faire market philosophy. Smith warns that restraining free competition does not always come about by "corporate law", but rather by the behavior of "merchants".

As he put it "people of the same trade seldom meet together, even for merriment and diversion, but the conversation ends in a conspiracy against the public, or in some contrivance to raise prices." He goes on to state that "it is impossible indeed to prevent such meetings, by law," but the law "ought to do nothing" to facilitate such accessibility" (p.128).

Next Smith turns to the determination of the return to land, or rent.

If one thinks of land as the stock that enters the production process as an input then the return to that stock is the profit, or interest, that has to be paid for the use of the stock. Smith offered the following propositions:

- The rent paid to landowners is a monopoly price. As such, it is not proportional to the investment made for the improvements in the use of the land; neither does it depend on what the owner can "afford" to take, or the user to "give".
- Rent as a component of the price of the commodity differs from both the wage and profit in that a high or low profit and a high or low wage affect the price of commodities, whereas the rent is residual; high or low rent depends on the price of the commodities.

- Rent depends on the quality of the land in use: more fertile land commands a higher rent and vice versa.
- Easy access and location increase the rent, as well as the type of produce of the land: the easy the transport, the higher is the rent.
- An increase in the wealth of society as well as an increase in the labor employed with the land will indirectly increase the rent.

Malthus on Returns to Factors

Unlike Smith, Malthus in his volume *On Population* does not address the demand for factors or the returns to factors, as those were not his main issues of concern. As we pointed out earlier in the chapter, Malthus was greatly disturbed about the imbalance between the growth of the population (the laboring class in particular) and the growth of food, or subsistence. This concern, although it might have been justified at that time and place (eighteenth century England), was unwarranted, if not exaggerated. Moreover, this preoccupation with population dominated his essays, so much that it was difficult to extrapolate from them a theory of returns to factors or a theory of production.

Malthus nonetheless did offer insights into the demand for labor, the cost of maintaining labor (subsistence), and the supply of labor. Of interest is the link Malthus saw between the price of corn and the insistence of consumers (laboring class) on obtaining the good. This insistence is what we refer to today as elasticity of demand. In this example, the behavior of labor that Malthus observed characterizes an "inelastic" demand for foodstuff.

With these remarks about Malthus's preoccupation with the population issue in relation to food supply, there are nonetheless a few principles that he put forward regarding the demand for labor and the returns (wages) of the laboring class. These principles are given below:

- The price of labor (the wage rate) is governed by two elements: the supply of provisions and the number of consumers.

This principle embodies several relations while neglecting others. First, the tie-in between the wage rate paid labor and the supply of provisions, namely subsistence, suggests that the value of labor services does not enter into the determination of the price of labor. Secondly, the dependence of the wage rate for labor services on the number of consumers of the provisions initially appears a bit out of place. However, if one were to take the number of consumers as a proxy of the total demand (quantity demanded) for the provisions, then Malthus's principle may be restated more accurately as follows:

- The price of labor depends on the price of provisions.

This restatement of the principle captures both the aggregate demand and aggregate supply of provision and thus relates the price of labor to the price of provision. In effect, later on in his volume Malthus links the price of labor and the price of provisions by stating the following:

"When an advance in the price of provisions already expresses that the demand is too great for the supply, in order to put the labourer in the same condition as before, we raise the price of labour" (Malthus, 1969 Ed., p. 63).

However, Malthus believed that the rise in the price of labor is self-defeating, as the price of provisions will continue to rise. Where this does leave labor? His response: To the "poor house" surely. This is probably why the English had the so-called the "poor laws".

A second principle advanced by Malthus posits an inverse relationship between wages and employment, especially the employment of the laboring class:

- It is an absolute impossibility that all different classes of society should be well paid and fully employed, if the supply of labor exceeds the demand (p.385).

Clearly when the supply of labor exceeds demand, the wage rate has to fall. Malthus acknowledges this outcome, by stating that when the demand for labor falls short of supply, either "all" wages fall or a great number of workers would be "thrown out" of their employment. He modified this statement by singling out the low classes of workers, the laboring class who, according to Malthus, would suffer an increasing poverty and distress.

Malthus then linked the price of commodities to the wage rate and employment of labor as follows:

- A rise in the price of commodities not accompanied by a rise in the money wage of labor is more than counterbalanced by the increase in the employment of labour (p.463).
- A fall in prices does not necessarily lead to a proportionate fall in wages. The fall in prices more often is counterbalanced by a fall in the demand for labor.

Concerns for the conditions of the laboring class would suggest that a remedy would be prescribed where provisions would be increased in proportion to the number of consumers. This solution however, according to Malthus is self-defeating. As he put it, "As fast as this is done, the number of consumers more than kept up the pace with it." This state was portrayed by Malthus as a race between the tortoise and the hare:

"Finding therefore that from the law of nature, we could not proportion the food to the population; our next attempt should be to proportion the population to the food." The problem would be solved, according to Malthus, if the hare can be persuaded to go to sleep, so that the tortoise may have a chance to overtake the hare (p.560).

His voluminous inquiry into the principles of population led Malthus to suggest that nothing much can be done to improve the condition of the laboring class. Upward mobility is completely beyond their reach. As he put it: "A stricter inquiry into the principles of population obliges us to conclude that we shall never be able to throw down the ladder by which we have risen to this eminence" (p.593). Put differently, there is no chance for the laboring class to rise beyond their status.

It is not surprising that Malthus saw no way out of the imbalance between nature forces; population versus foodstuff. The solution seems to rest with the population—the laboring class. One gleans this conviction from the following passage: "The cause that has the most lasting effect in improving the situation of the lower classes of society depends chiefly upon the conduct and prudence of the individual themselves, and is therefore not immediately and necessarily connected with an increase in the means of subsistence" (p.455).

David Ricardo on the Returns to Factors

Ricardo's essays on the returns to factors (chapters II, IV, V and VI), follow a tradition set forth by Smith in assigning two values to the returns to the factors of production: a natural price and a market price. The use of the term natural price originated with the Physiocrats, who put forth the thesis that the return to labor is the natural price of labor, an amount barely sufficient to maintain labor. That is, it is a level below subsistence.

Although the concept of a natural price of labor, as posited by the Physiocrats has been discredited (it may even be said that it has led to discarding their views about the economy), it has remained in the writings of Smith, Ricardo, and Mill, as well as Marshall.

Ricardo's discussion of wages and the return to labor begins by stating that "labour" like other things which are traded has its natural and market price. He defines the natural price as that which enables labor to reproduce itself, which is to say it has to cover subsistence and reproduction. Ricardo, like Smith before him, ties in the natural price of labor to the price of subsistence and necessaries of life.

Next, Ricardo defines a market price for labor. Again like Smith, this price is said to be determined by the demand and supply of labor. The market price rises when labor is dear, falls when labor is plentiful.

Of interest, is the relation Ricardo hypothesized between the market price and the natural price for labor. Given that the natural price is that which is just enough to enable labor to reproduce itself, it follows that if the market price for labor were to exceed this subsistence level, labor conditions would improve, labor flourishes. The opposite leads to "deprivation" (p.94).

Ricardo focused next on sources that would improve the market price of labor. One such source is capital, where capital is the part of wealth, which is employed in production. This capital is necessary to improve the effectiveness of labor, hence its market price, as well as the quantity of labor used to produce additional supply of goods, such as food, clothing, and the like. On the other hand, an increase in the use of capital may not increase the market price for labor if capital use had a substitution effect; more goods are produced with reduced amount of labor.

The link between the market price for labor and the natural price of labor is always present in Ricardo's exposition. If the use of capital impacted the price of subsistence, then the condition of labor would improve or deteriorate depending on whether the price of subsistence falls or rises. Ricardo emphasizes this point often—the variation in the price of food and necessaries. This variation is said to exist at all times and for all countries (p.96). In short, the determination of wages is said to depend on two sources: The demand and supply of labor and the price of the commodities on which the wages of labor are spent. As mentioned above, the first determines the market price, the second the natural price.

Ricardo did not pursue the diversion between the market price and the natural price, except to point out that if the market price were to fall in magnitude such that labor could not afford to maintain itself, this situation would give rise to poverty and a fall in their numbers. What happens, if an imbalance were to exist between the number of people and the quantity of food and necessaries of life? This is the kind of question that dominated Malthus's thesis on population.

Ricardo also had a solution to this imbalance: "With a population pressing against the means of subsistence, the only remedies are either a reduction of people or a rapid accumulation of capital" (p.99).

The idea that the accumulation of capital may solve the food shortages problem does not get Ricardo out of the box he found himself in. As mentioned above, he sees capital as replacing labor, and thus causing the wage bill to shrink and the market price of labor to fall. The only way out of this box is when the fall in the market price of labor has been accompanied by a fall in the natural price of labor, i.e. the price of food and necessaries of life.

This may not be untenable since the use of capital is said to increase the production of such goods and hence their prices would fall. Unfortunately, Ricardo did not pursue further the link between the use of capital and the efficiency of labor, and/or the relative effect of capital accumulation on the market price of labor vis-à-vis the natural price of labor. Moreover, Ricardo did not explain why, the advancement of society (presumably with the increase of capital accumulation), should have an adverse effect on labor. As he put it, "In the natural advance of society, the wages of labour will have a tendency to fall, as far they regulated by supply and demand, for the supply of labour will continue to increase at the same rate, whilst the demand for them will increase at a slower rate" (p.104).

A principle governing the wage rate may be stated as follows:

- An increase in society's wealth and capital, when they give rise to an increase demand for labor, will increase the production of commodities.

From this, it follows that an increase in the wealth of a nation and the accumulation of capital would make it possible for a rise in the demand for labor and a higher production of goods, and presumably a fall in the price of necessaries.

The Returns to Land: Rent

Ricardo defines rent as "the portion of the produce of earth, which is paid to the landlord for the use of the original and indestructible power of the soil" (p.65). This is by far the most restrictive definition of rent, which Ricardo insists is the correct one. As in the tradition of English economists such as Smith and Mill, Ricardo began his exposition of the determination of land rent by taking issue with Adam Smith's position as to what constitutes land rent.

According to Ricardo, Smith's concept of rent embodies more than what rent supposed to be. "He [Smith] tells us, that the demand for timber and its subsequent high price, in the more southern countries of Europe, caused a rent to be paid for forests in Norway, which could before afford no rent." This critique is in line with Ricardo's own narrow definition of what constitutes rent.

Thus, from the laws of supply and demand Ricardo's principles may be stated:

- No rent would be paid if there is abundance of land.
- Rent depends on land scarcity and its quality.

Ricardo next addressed the impact of land quality on land rent. Because land has different qualities, land use begins with land of good quality and progresses as demand for land services increases to the use of land with lower (inferior) quality. But land in the production process requires the use of other factors of production to produce products. Therefore, Ricardo introduces the services of capital applied to land to obtain the produce. Since capital use adds to the product of land, Ricardo makes the argument that "inferior" land should not be used if the land product can be augmented with the use of capital. Since capital can be employed more productively (increases land product), capital use creates land rent. Given that two factors of production, labor, and capital are applied to land, what the landowner receives, land rent, depends on the quality of land and scarcity of land. Thus:

- When good land exists in a quantity more than sufficient to produce food for an increasing population, there could be no rise in rent.
- If capital could be employed in conjunction with land without diminishing returns, there would be no rise in rent.
- Application of additional units of capital, or labor (equal size units), to a fixed piece of land results into diminishing returns.
- The exchangeable value of all commodities, whether they be manufactured or the product of land, is determined by the most unfavorable circumstances under which the product is produced (marginal unit).
- When land is most abundant, most productive, and most fertile, it yields no rent.
- Infertile land put in production yields less returns to labor, but it also give rise to rent on fertile land.
- Rent does not enter as a component of the price of commodities.
- Whatever diminishes the difference in the produce obtained from successive amounts of capital employed on the same unit of land tends to reduce rent; whatever increases this

difference has the opposite effect. The return from capital of the poorest land regulates the rent for all other more productive land and tends to increase the rent.

The third factor of production is the stock of capital whose returns needed to be determined.

In chapter VI Ricardo advances the following proposition: the rate of profit is variable. The question that needs to be addressed then is what accounts for this variability.

The presumption there was that the whole value of a commodity is divided between two components: profits on the stock and the wages of labor. The assumption made was that no rent is paid by the farmer (the producer of the commodities); rather it falls on the consumers of the commodities. Ricardo exposition suggests that the farmer is the owner of the stock (p.114).

An inverse relationship was stated by Ricardo between the price of the good produced by the farmer (for example corn) and the money value of the farmer's profit. This inverse relationship stems from the fact that a rise in the price of corn increases the money wage paid to laborer, thus reducing the farmer's profit.

Rent was treated as residual; after the payments for wages and profits, the leftovers could be paid as rent. Whether wages or profits were to rise or fall, the value of the produce is the one that determines the returns to labor and to capital. There again a link is established between returns to the two factors: profits fall when wages are rising and vice versa. What precipitates the rise of wages is the price of the necessaries. Again, Ricardo links profit to wages through the change in the price of "necessaries". From this we may derive the following principles governing the rate of profits:

- The rise of wages is necessitated by the rise in the price of necessaries, and as a consequence to this rise, profits fall.
- The downward gravitation of profits is kept in check at repeated intervals by the improvement in the elements of production as well as by discoveries in the science of agriculture (technical innovation).
- Technical advances and capital accumulation reduce the amount of labor required to produce a given output, and

thus wages fall. The inverse relationship between wages and profits would guarantee that profits would increase as wage payments fall (pp.289-300).

Ricardo was, however, careful to point out that this result may not always hold. Capital accumulation may work the other way on the rate of profit. As he explained: "we should also expect that the rate of profits on the stock might diminish in consequence of the accumulation of capital on land (diminishing returns) and the rise of wages." Nonetheless, he argued that the total profits might still increase, but at a decreasing rate. He concluded by emphasizing some of the principles stated earlier as follows:

- The rise of wages would not necessarily raise the price of commodities, but would invariably reduce profits.
- A rise in the price of all commodities would have the same effect on profits.

Much of the discussion as stated above had to do with the accumulation of the stock on profits. With respect to interest, Ricardo advanced the proposition that, though ultimately and permanently the rate of interest is governed by the rate of profit, it is however subject to temporary variations due to the fluctuation in the quantity of money (p.297). Given that commodities prices vary with the change in the quantity and the value of money as well as with their supply and demand, prices fall with an abundant supply, from a fall in demand or from a rise in the value of money. As the market price of goods fall, a manufacturer will accumulate a great quantity of finished goods, as he would be unwilling to sell his goods at depressed prices. To meet his payments, he would need to borrow, and this would raise the interest rate.

John Stuart Mill on the Returns to Factors

Mill like his predecessors, Smith and Ricardo, began his essay on the principles of economics with the theory of production. To discuss a production process, it is essential for an outline of a theory to enumerate those factors that are engaged in the production process.

Factors of production are known, but their returns have to be postulated. It is common knowledge that the factors of production are labor, capital, and land. Sometimes a fourth factor, the entrepreneur, is added as a separate agent of production, but until modern economic literature assigned a separate role to the entrepreneur, it has been seldom analyzed as a fourth factor with positive returns separate from the returns to labor.

In Book I, chapters I through XIV (Mill, 1969 Ed) 197 pages are devoted to an analysis of the returns to these factors, their contribution to the production process, as well as to their returns. Labor as a factor of production is discussed in chapter I. There, he defines labors' function and their contribution to the supply of commodities. Of interest is the similarity between Mill and Smith in that Mill recognizes two factors of production, namely labor and nature. Thus, he like Smith (as well as other classical economists), was to view the third factor, namely capital as the embodiment of labor and technology.

The Return to Labor

Labor, according to Mill, possesses two elements: bodily labor and mental labor. Bodily labor refers to physical capabilities whereas mental labor includes such things as feelings, annoyance as well as one's thoughts (p.22). Although mental labor exerts influence on the ability of a laborer to perform whatever function assigned to him, physical labor seems to be what defines the productivity of labor. As Mill put it, labor is needed to transform materials supplied by nature into objects for use, i.e. "nature supplies materials and labor transforms them" (p.25).

Mill segmented labor into two categories: Productive labor and unproductive labor (see Smith above). Productive labor is defined as that which confers "productive power" whereas unproductive labor does not contribute to the production of goods and services (pp.34-37).

Unproductive labor, a term of disparagement, refers to any labor that produces no benefit or pleasure worth the cost. This describes, according to Mill, "the labor of officers of government, of the army and navy, of physicians, lawyers, teachers and musicians, dancers, actors, domestic labours and so forth". When they accomplish what they are paid for, they may be labeled unproductive in the sense that, their labor does not terminate in the creation of wealth (p.49). In short, unproductive labor may be as useful or more so as productive labor, but it cannot be considered productive unless it adds to the stock of the material wealth.

In the introductory chapter, Mill emphasizes the fact that the value of labor (labor services) upon which the rewards for labor are determined cannot be separated out from the contribution of other factors (such as land and capital) employed in the production of commodities (see Marshall below on this point). In chapter XI however, Mill offered a theory on wage determination and the factors that influence their determination. These factors are customs and competition. Competition exerts the most influence, whereas customs may be considered as "modifying circumstances". These factors none withstanding, the essence of Mill analyses regarding wage determination rests on the fundamentals of the supply and demand for labor.

Mill recognized the contribution of capital in setting laborers' wages through its enhancement of output. Given that both capital and land are used in the production of many goods, the demand for labor will depend on the demand for goods that require the application of both capital and land.

The supply of labor will depend on the wage offered, which in turn depends on the contribution of labor to the values of the commodities as well. One other factor recognized by Mill as determining wages is the so-called "wage fund". This is the fund set aside by capitalists to pay labor wages.

Mill glanced over the factors that affect both the supply and demand of labor, to address the question of the remuneration of labor in different employment. One of the reasons given by Mill for the inequality of wages in different types of employment is job-specific—that is, differences in the wage paid reflect "disagreeableness" of employment. Thus, he postulates:

- Inequality of remunerations is necessary to produce equality of attractiveness.

Another reason given for the differences in wages is differences in labor skills; "desirable labour, those whom everyone is anxious to have" receive higher remuneration than unskilled labor (p.388). By way of concluding his discussion of labor returns, he went back to his earlier statement that custom and competition determines wages.

According to Mill, in cases where a labor monopoly exists rather than competition, then wages could be kept above the competitive rate. Where wages are fixed by custom, such as the fees charged by professional persons, wages paid are likely not to change through competition (p.404).

Returns to Capital

The starting point in the analysis is to define the term capital. According to Mill, "capital is the accumulated stock of the product of former labour". This definition is in line with Smith's definition presented above, in which he attributed the origin of capital to the accumulation of past labor. Capital is a factor of production like labor and land; although it differs from both in that it supplies the funds from which labor is paid.

Mill in essence lumps together real capital, business equipment, and materials with "nominal" or money capital used by the capitalist to pay for the services of the other factors employed in production. "I have assumed that the labourers are always subsisted from capital; and this is obscured the facts" (Mill, 1968 Ed, p.58).

Capital is classified into two categories: fixed capital and circular capital. Another category that is not much explored is the stock of finished unsold goods or inventory. Fixed capital consists of machinery, tools, and the like, whereas circulating capital is that which is used up in the production process. Fixed capital depreciates and needs to be replaced, whereas circular capital is exhausted in use. Mill offered the following propositions with regards the use of capital:

- Industry is limited by the amount of the stock of capital.

- Capital may be temporarily unemployed due to lack of investment opportunities.
- All capital was originally the result of saving.
- What supports and employs labor is capital.

The Returns to Capital: Profits

According to Mill, the capitalist advances the whole expense of production including the remuneration of labor, thus he receives all the produce. His profits, then, consist of the "excess of the produce above the advances"; it is the "ratio which that excess bears to the advancement" (p.418).

Two elements determine capitalists' profits: the amount of produce and the proportion of the produce obtained by laborers. Mill, like Ricardo, relates the capitalists' profit to labor remunerations as follows:

- The rate of profit will depend on the cost of labor employed in production.

This postulate, according to Mill, differs from Ricardo's statement that profits depend on the size of wages, thus implying that labor costs are not the same as labor wages.

Returns to Land, or Rent

"The Theory of rent is one of the cardinal doctrines of political economy—it has been denied that there can be any land in cultivation that pays no rent" (p.425).

This proposition is fundamental for understanding the determination of the returns to land. As stated earlier, Mill argued that the prerequisites of production are labor and nature.

Land is the principal of the natural agents that are capable of being appropriated, and what is paid for its use is called rent. Rent, in a sense, is the effect of a monopoly.

The reason why land owners require rent is that it is a commodity that many want, and which no one can obtain but from these owners. Different land characteristics give rise to differences in rent.

According to Mill, the rent of all land is measured by the excess of the return to the capital employed on it, over and above what the capital would yield if it were employed in the least productive part. In some sense, rent is a surplus value; poor land brought into cultivation yields no rent.

An increase in the application of labor and capital to land (land being fixed), gives rise to diminishing returns. This is explained fully by Ricardo, and thus Mill did not devote much to explain this outcome. He only noted that because of differences in the fertility of land, there will be some land used in cultivation that pays no rent. Thus the following proposition may be stated:

- The land in cultivation which yields least return to labor and capital employed on it gives only the ordinary profit of capital, without leaving anything for rent (p.425).
- Rent is the excess of its produce beyond what would be returned to the same capital if employed on the worst land in cultivation.

Leon Walras on the Returns to Factors

Walras formulated a theory of production, and on the basis of the demand and supply of factors, solved for factor prices. Given that his framework is a general equilibrium framework, the determination of all variables is arrived at through the simultaneous interactions in the goods and factor markets.

To simplify the presentation, we extract from the mathematical model those elements that shed light on the determination of supply and the returns to factors of production. Just as a market was needed for determining the price of final products (the goods market), Walras considered a market, which he called "a capital goods market," where capital goods are bought and sold.

Walras begins by posing the question: *Why are capital goods demanded?* As such goods are not consumed in the normal sense (consumer goods); they are demanded because of the services they rendered. These services are: land services, capital services, and labor services. It is worth emphasizing at this juncture that Walras designates any factor that yields services as capital goods; hence, labor is treated as a capital good in the same way as land or the stock of capital. Accordingly, the price of a capital good depends on the price of its services—on its income. On the basis of this postulate, Walras formulated the following principle:

- The values of capital goods are proportional to their income.

Walras draws an analogy between the market for goods and the market for factors of production. He argues that in formulating a theory of exchange, the analysis usually begins with an exchange of two commodities (in-kind exchange) and/or exchanges of several commodities through the medium of money. But commodities are products that are produced with the services of the factors of production such as labor, land, and capital services. Thus, a theory of production has to be developed to determine the cost (the cost price) of these commodities.

Before outlining his theory of production, Walras needed to classify those capital services: those that are fixed and durable and those that are not. In this classification, he distinguishes between income and capital. Anything that is durable is capital; anything that is not durable is income.

Walras's choice of this terminology derives from the fact that anything that outlasts the first use which is made of it provides services lasting more than one period and hence constitutes capital; anything that does not outlast the first use is treated as income. Thus, according to Walras, the distinction between capital and income is fundamental for the development of a theory of production and credit. Next he classifies the factors according to ownership: a holder of land is a landowner; a holder of "personal faculties" is a worker; and a holder of capital is a capitalist.

In formulating a production theory wherein the production process requires the use of more than one factor, factor combinations, or ratios, have to be decided upon. In doing so, Walras introduces a new element in the production process: the entrepreneur whose function is to direct the production process and determine factor ratios. The concept of an entrepreneur is to be distinguished from that of a worker. In his role as an entrepreneur, he acts in two markets; the first is the services market, and the second is the product market. For production purposes, the entrepreneur deals in the first market.

In the services market, landowners, workers, and capitalists act as sellers, while the entrepreneurs act as buyers of these services. In the same market, these three factors also act as buyers of services for consumption. In the services market, where services of labor, land, and capital are offered, the exchange takes place with the aid of a "numeraire" (money), under the assumption of perfect competition.

At this competitive price, if the demand exceeds the effective offer, the entrepreneurs will bid against each other, and the price of factor services will rise; if the effective offer exceeds the demand, the factors of production (landowners, laborer, and capitalists) will bid against each other and the price for their services will fall. The equilibrium price is one that equates the effective demand with the effective offer. From this presentation, the principles governing the demand and supply of factors can be stated as follows:

- The effective demand and the effective offer set the correct (equilibrium) price of factor services.

In the second market—the product or goods market—the entrepreneurs act as sellers whereas the factors of production, landowners, laborers, and capitalists act as buyers. In the same manner as in the case of the services market, perfect competition prevails so that the competitive price is established through competitive bidding.

Equilibrium in production as outlined above also is equilibrium in exchange. This equilibrium may be stated as follows:

- It is a state where effective demand and effective offer of productive services are equal, and there exists a stationary price in the market for these services.

- It is a state where the effective demand and effective supply of products (goods) are equal and there exists a stationary price in the product market.
- It is a stationary state where the selling prices of products equal their cost of productive services that are used in the production process.

From these three propositions, it is clear that the first two conditions describe the equilibrium in exchange, whereas the third relates to equilibrium in production.

Walras was careful to emphasize the fact that the equilibrium conditions stated above describe an ideal state and not a real state. Hence, he put forth the concept of "disequilibrium," which he defined as a state that may prevail in both the product and the services markets. As he put it, "It never happens in the real world that the selling price of any given product is absolutely equal to the cost of the productive services that enter into that product, or that the effective demand and supply of services or products are absolutely equal."

Having clarified the concept of equilibrium, he added that equilibrium in the normal state is a state, towards that which things spontaneously tend towards under a regime of free competition in exchange and production.

An important market characteristic that defines free competition is the free entry and exit. Under free competition, if the selling price of a product were to exceed the cost of the productive services for some firms, then entrepreneurs will flock toward this type of product and expand output, so that the increase in the quantity pushes the price downward, reducing the difference between the price and the cost, and vice versa if the rise in price was not sufficient to cover the cost. Walras then defines equilibrium in production as:

- Equilibrium in production is a state where neither profit nor loss exists.

Given that Walras enumerated returns to only three factors—landowners, labor and capital—the question arises as to the entrepreneur's return. There he states that the entrepreneur receives compensation in his capacity as owner of a factor of production and not as an entrepreneur. As posited above, it is clear that Walras's views differed greatly from his predecessors' views, in that neither Smith nor Ricardo discussed explicitly the services of the fourth factor, the entrepreneur.

Marshall on Production and the Returns to factors

"Human agents of production are not bought and sold as machinery and other materials". Labor power is perishable, that the sellers of it are commonly poor and have no reserve fund, and that they cannot easily withhold it from the market. (Marshall, 1948 Ed, p.527).

Marshall in Book IV, chapter I, began the discussion of the agents (factors) of production by defining the following terms: land is the "materials and the forces of nature"; labour is "the economic work of man"; and capital is "all stored up provisions," including material goods and knowledge needed for the production of material goods.

Having enumerated the traditional factors, labor, land, and capital, Marshall posits that if we think about these agents of production, we come up with the proposition that there exist only two factors of productions: labor and nature. Capital is the creation of man's knowledge in conjunction of the forces of nature (p.138).

In Book IV, chapters I and II, Marshall presented extensive treatises on the returns to factors engaged in the production of commodities. He began first with a discussion of what he called a "preliminary survey of the distribution of the national income". In this survey he provided a chronicle of the determination of wages from the writing of the Physiocrats to that of John Stuart Mill.

As articulated by Marshall, the main thesis put forth by the Physiocrats was that there was something like the "natural law" or "necessary" rate of profit that corresponds to the "natural rate of wages". Given that wages and profits are fixed by natural laws, it follows that the value of everything was governed by the sum of profits and wages required to compensate the producers.

Recall that in chapter 2 of this volume, we pointed out that the Physiocrats' thesis petered out, as Smith and other English economists have argued that natural laws do not govern the determination of wages and profits, and that the assumption of the existence of such a natural link is not valid.

The idea that some kind of law prevailed that fixes the wage rate was also advanced by Ricardo. As we saw earlier in the chapter, Ricardo did suggest the existence of some kind of law that fixes the market price of labor. This law ties in wages not to profits but to the cost of food and necessaries of life. And, as he put it, as soon as the wages rose above the necessaries of life, population increased and that causes wages to be fixed by a "natural law".

This law, according to Marshall, has been called, especially in Germany, Ricardo's "iron" or "brazen" law. Marshall was to point out, however, that Ricardo seemed reluctant to insist on the existence of such a law, although he had repeatedly suggested that as soon as wages rise, population would increase, which would in turn cause wages to fall, thereby fixing wages to the value of necessaries of life (p.508).

As discussed above, the focus for Smith, Malthus, and Ricardo has always been on the determination of wages, or the market price of labor and not so much on the factors that determines the demand and supply of labor. This omission has been addressed by Marshall.

Marshall in Book IV, chapter III, began with a review of earlier theses regarding labor remuneration. This review was needed so that he could decouple the determination of the wage rate from the rate of profit and or the "necessaries of life". For Marshall, the forces that determine the rate of return for a factor of production must ultimately emanate from the market demand and supply of that factor, the efficiency of the work as well as the efficiency of capital used in the production of commodities. Of note is that this proposition was intended to apply not only to labor in the production process, but also to all factors employed.

According to Marshall, "the uses of each agent of production are governed by the general conditions of demand and in relation to supply" (p.520). The quality of a factor contribution to the production outcome is maintained by the constant reallocation of the factor away from usage where the factor is less efficient to others factors' services, which are of the greatest value in accordance with the principles of substitution. In other words, marginal uses and marginal efficiency of the factors of production must be monitored as the factor reward or return is determined by it—that is, the efficiency of a factor in production is the measure of its earning.

The Marginal Efficiency of a Factor of Production

Marshall established a criterion for evaluating the contribution of a factor of production to the final product or commodities. This criterion is the so-called marginal efficiency of the factor in a given use or employment. This concept had implications as well for the allocation of a factor among various uses so that the factor would be employed in the activity that yields the highest return. But what determine this efficiency?

Marshall identified two elements that would account for factors' efficiency: the first is what he called, the "immediate solution," and the second is the "relative solution". The first is related to the available supply of the factor, while the second requires an understanding of what determines supply. Knowledge of the available supply of a factor signals the degree to which that factor would be used as well as the type of usage: "for if the supply is increased, the thing (factor) will be applied to uses for which it is less needed, and in which it is less efficient". In other words, the supply of a factor impacts its efficiency given the opportunity available for its use.

With respect to the second criterion, the argument put forth by Marshall was that knowledge of the causes that determine the supply of a factor signal not only the level of stock available of that factor but also its willingness to offer it. Based on these propositions the following principles may be put forth:

- The production of any thing is carried out up to the margin at which there is equilibrium between the forces of supply and demand.
- The effective supply of any factor of production at any point in time depends on the available stock of that factor, as well as on factor's willingness to offer it in production.
- The willingness of a factor of production to participate in the production process is not governed by the immediate return,

which the factor expects, as there may be a lower limit below which work will not be offered.

- An increase in the return to labor causes an immediate increase in supply. Exception to this does exist, where a higher wage leads to a reduction in work. (this phenomenon is referred to in modern economics as backward bending supply schedule of labor).

The demand and supply of labor exert coordinate effect on the wage rate.

Wages tend to equal the marginal product of labor, whereas the demand price of labor is determined by its marginal productivity.

Although wages, in Marshall's view, tend to be closely but indirectly related to the cost of training, rearing, and sustaining the energy of efficient labor, the wage offer does not reflect these costs. Wages were neither determined by the demand price nor the supply price of labor, rather they were determined by all the factors that govern the supply and demand for labor.

Marshall then turned to the analyses of the efficiency of the worker, which according to him govern the wage offer. To begin with, he addresses the environment where labor services are offered, as such an environment would likely influence wages. Equality of the wage rate in the various employment of labor was said to depend on market condition; that economic freedom and freedom of enterprise tend to equalize the wages in occupations of similar difficulty; that is occupations requiring the same level of efforts (or disutility).

From this characterization, Marshall assigned the label of "efficiency wages," to designate the equalization of wages paid to workers in use requiring the same level of effort "exertion of ability and efficiency required of the worker" (p.549). The tendency for wage equalization in the occupation with similar difficulties is stronger the greater is the mobility of labor and the less specialized they were. From these propositions we may derive the following two principles:

- The more mobile and less specialized labor is the more likely that wages are equalized in similar use.
- Wages paid to labor depends on the type of employment; the more irregular is the occupation, the higher the pay (p.555).

On Land Rent

According to Marshall, the theory of rent of land is not an "isolated economic doctrine, but merely one of the chief applications of a particular corollary for the general theory of supply and demand" (p.629). This statement is the most fundamental proposition that has been advanced (repeatedly) by Marshall as to the determination of factor returns.

Having postulated that rent is determined by the forces of supply and demand, Marshall devoted two chapters to a discussion of a concept (land rent) that has been addressed previously by Smith, Ricardo, and Mill. As will be discussed below, Marshall took great pains in pointing out some of the errors in Ricardo's analysis of rent, in particular his discussion of the concept of diminishing returns, although he seemed to agree with Mill's exposition on the subject of rent.

Marshall first needed to define what land is, in economic sense, through a definition of its attributes. According to Marshall, land is said to possess attributes whose supply is not dependent on human effort. These attributes clearly include location, fertility, and other environment-specific attributes. Other attributes, however, are subject to modification through man's efforts—scientific advances in agriculture, for example, can include irrigation and soil improvements as well as the application of capital in cultivation.

Herein lies the problem that Ricardo has alluded to in his analysis of land rent—the law of, or statement of, the tendency toward diminishing returns. This tendency or law has become identified as Ricardo's law of "diminishing marginal return to land" (DMR). Marshall was also of the view that Ricardo's law does hold: "An increase in the capital and labor applied in the cultivation of land causes in general "a less than proportional increase" in the amount of produce" (p.150).

The law of diminishing return seems to have been recognized long before Marshall himself expounded upon the subject: "This tendency to diminishing return was the cause of Abraham's parting from Lot and of most of the migration of which history tells" (p.151).

Marshall nonetheless insisted that Ricardo's law of diminishing returns should be viewed as a tendency, as there exists circumstances where an increase in the use of labor and capital on land (land is assumed to be fixed) would not necessarily, at least for quite sometimes give rise to diminishing returns. Indeed, at least for a while, with the successive application of labor and capital, increasing rather than decreasing returns may be observed. To further clarify how the tendency toward diminishing returns arises, Marshall borrowed John Stuart Mill's designation of the units of labor and capital applied to land by modifying the tendency statement as follows:

Capital and labor applied to land as consisting of equal successive doses may give rise to increasing return. But a point will be reached after which all doses will lead to a less than proportionate return than the preceding doses. The dose is the combined dose of labor and capital. According to Marshall, the dose that only "remunerates" the cultivator may be said to be the "marginal dose," and the return to it is a "marginal return" (p.153). The marginal return is that which is just sufficient to remunerate the cultivator. From this definition, it follows that the cultivator will be just remunerated for the value of the capital and labor by as many times the marginal return as he has applied doses" (p.155). Thus, the amount that is in excess of this remuneration is known as the surplus produce. The surplus is retained by the cultivator if he was the owner of the land.

It is worth noting that Marshall emphasized the notion that the surplus is not rent. The producer's surplus of land is not of the "greatness of the bounty of nature, it is evidence of the limitations of that bounty". If the supply of land were unlimited, a surplus would not occur.

The Returns to Capital, Interest, and Profit

Marshall turned next to the returns to another agent of production: interest and profit. The analysis appears in Book VI, chapters VI and VII.

It is worth noting from the start that Marshall, unlike his forerunner Smith and Ricardo, attributed two types of returns to capital: interest and profits. Accordingly, he saw fit to provide a historical background about interest payments being a return to the use of the stock of capital.

First, he advanced the notion that capital use must yield a return: "Everyone is aware that no payment would be offered for the use of capital unless some gains were expected from that use." Secondly, he enumerated such uses of capital building homes, machinery, structures, manufactured goods, and so on. These uses must yield something to whomever utilizes the capital; otherwise capital would not be utilized. Most significant, is Marshall's insistence that no one would lend own capital "gratis".

This Marshallian view was outside the mainstream of the economic doctrines from medieval' history that ended at the time of Adam Smith and David Ricardo. In refuting this mainstream position, Marshall referred to Aristotle as saying that "money is barren," and that to derive a return, interest from lending it out, was to put it to an "unnatural use". Medieval writers, following Aristotle's lead according to Marshall, argued that if the "loan of capital to the borrower cost the lender nothing if the lender had no use of it himself, then he is bound to lend it "gratis"."

Marshall undoubtedly disagreed with this assessment. He correctly points out that this doctrine did convey to the people the fallacy that the loan of money or the command of money over commodities does not involve a sacrifice. What needed to be articulated is that the lender gives up the power of use over his money (capital). If this were not true, then the services of capital would be free, and the question of the motives for capital accumulation would arise.

Marshall is credited for this insight into the requirement that payment (interest) is owed to the lender by the borrower for the use of his capital. Thus, he defined interest as the "earning of capital simply," or the "reward of capital simply," as *net* interest. Once defined, the next task before him was to put forth the determination of the rate of interest.

According to Marshall, "Interest, being the price paid for the use of capital in any market, tends towards an equilibrium level such that the aggregate demand for capital in the market, at that rate of interest, is equal to the aggregate stock forthcoming there at that rate" (p.534). The term interest, however, includes other elements, thus, it was labeled gross interest.

Several elements to Marshall's analysis of interest need to be stressed. One of these elements involves the payment of interest as a return for the postponement of the use of capital by the lender. What is involved there is the issue of "time preference". The postponement of the use of funds involves a postponement of present consumption for future consumption. And in view of the fact that people show a tendency for preference of present consumption over future consumption, a payment would have to be offered to the lender to forego present consumption, with the promise that he will be able to acquire upon repayment a bigger fund that could be used for future consumption.

The time preference, the present versus future consumption became the cornerstone in the modern analysis of inter-temporal utility functions.

In addition to the net interest that needed to be paid to compensate the lender for the postponement of the use of his capital, Marshall argued that there is an extra premium that needs to be paid, a "risk premium" to compensate the lender for the decline of the value of money due to inflation (a rise in the general price level). If this component was not allowed for, then the lender would receive a lower value for the loan expressed in terms of the purchasing power of money. Another type of risk is that of "borrower's default" on the loan, in the event that the demand for his businesses falters or for some other reason the borrower would be unable to pay the borrowed funds. The sum of net interest and the risk premiums, then, is the gross interest.

The next component as a return to capital is profits. There Marshall's exposition seems to echo Smith's view that labor constitutes national wealth. Accordingly, he posits that profits, for the most part, are the return to labor: "The greater part of the apparent profit is real wages disguised in the garb of profits" (p.608).

Marshall advanced the proposition that profits are of two types: a return to capital defined as the annual rates of profit on the capital invested in the business; the second type is the rate of profit as capital is turned over—a profit on the turnover of capital. Marshall emphasizes the fact that the forces that influence profits do not differ from those that influence wages.

As we saw earlier, Marshall had always advocated the principles of a market economy, where demand and supply forces determine the prices of all agents of productions as well as the price all commodities in exchange. Profits, hence, are no different in that their level is determined by market forces.

One characteristic that perhaps distinguishes the behavior of profits from wages is that profits are likely to be subject to much greater fluctuation than wages. One of the reasons accounting for this difference is that businesses are more likely to be exposed to greater risk in its operation than in those occupations where labor is employed. Another difference is that the profit of a business is much more affected by changes in its industrial environment and opportunity, although these changes may apply only to a limited degree to some workers skills.

Marshall concluded his discussion in his chapter on profit by making the observation that the employer in a business does not retain the whole gain (profit) of the business. In certain businesses there are specialized skills, and therefore the wage paid to those employees may consist partly of the "traditional" wage paid for the "fatigue" incurred by the work and partly of a "quasi-rent" of the workers' specialized skills. In short, there is *de facto* some sort of profit-loss sharing between businesses and their employees, hence the determination of business income or the income received by the business owner depends on the skill of their workers and the quasi rent.

Following analyses of the returns to factors, Marshall devoted several chapters to industrial organization, covering topics that were not discussed by Smith, Ricardo, or Mill. Moreover, except for Walras's essays on the simultaneous determination of supply and demand in both the commodities and factors markets, neither Smith nor Ricardo dedicated much time to the derivation of production costs, demand and supply functions for commodities or factors. This task fell to Marshall, who has provided extensive analyses of these economic concepts, which constitute what we refer to today as the study of microeconomics. Since the Marshallian analyses of these microeconomics concepts are covered in almost every text book on the principles of economics, we will not go into Marshall's exposition of cost, demand, and supply or the determination of prices in this chapter.

Summary

The literature survey presented above covers what we refer to today as principles of microeconomics. The historical review of the principles governing the private economy clearly show the diverse views held by the political economists of the eighteenth and nineteenth centuries. No matter how far back or how far forward one travels, however, a student of economics cannot but admire the thought processes that gave birth to the science of economics. As evidenced by our review, the science of economics emanated from the contributions of Adam Smith. The ideas of those who followed could not have been possible without in some way linking their own contributions to his.

As emphasized in the introduction to this volume, this survey aims to give the reader a glimpse of the origin of the principles of economics we often take for granted. Most importantly our aim in providing, this survey is to apprise students of economics of some of the issues that confronted the eighteenth and nineteenth century's political economists.

Rather than indulge in a survey of the literature (a good textbook on the history of economic thought would serve that purpose), what we aspired to do was to give students of economics a better understanding of the subject of economics through an understanding of the history of economic thought.

A few remarks about the political economists we have reviewed above: First, Adam Smith addressed the question of "what constitutes a Nation's wealth". To do so, he had to identify such a source; labor. Once identified, he dealt with the way society ought to harness and enhance this wealth. To accomplish these tasks, he put forth "principles" that should govern the goods market (consumers and producers), the labor and their employers in the factors market, and the "sovereign" (the state).

Political economists who followed Smith (the English School), in particular Malthus, Ricardo, Mill, and Marshall, performed two tasks: they first offered a critique of Smith's postulates (as well as those of political economists of earlier periods, notably the Mercantilists and the Physiocrats) and secondly, to put forth their own principles of the matter of economics.

Malthus's volume on population was chosen for our review, rather than his volume on Principles of Economics, as it was widely quoted because of its pessimistic appraisal of man's future. His thesis, simply put was that, there is a great deal of certainty that the growth of population left unchecked would outstrip the growth of food supply—referred to then as "subsistence and necessaries of life". Even though his gloomy prediction of this imbalance did not pan out, it did nonetheless underscore a possibility that needed to be explored to insure the "durability" and "augmentation" of Smith's wealth of the nation.

As we shall discuss in the next chapter, in conjunction with our review of principles which Keynes put forth in his *General Theory of Employment, Interest, and Money* 1936, Malthus may have in some way foreseen "ills" that could afflict future generations in general, but particularly the "labouring class".

Ricardo, Mill, and especially Marshall laid down the foundations of microeconomic analysis as we know it today in that they have advanced principles that govern individuals' behavior, in their roles as consumers, producers, and suppliers of factors of productions. In such endeavor they have put forth concepts such as efficiency wage, diminishing returns, diminishing marginal utility, the demand schedule, consumer surplus, the stability of equilibrium, and the stationary state to name but a few. Students of economics today take such concepts as the undisputed truth that defines human activities in the private economy.

Walras (of the French School), contribution differs from the English school's political economists discussed above both in term of "style" and by his insistence that a scientific inquiry cannot be carried out without the adoption of "mathematics", concepts and models.

Students of economics, especially in introductory classes are likely to shun teachers that use mathematics extensively in their class presentation. However, even at that level, the student cannot escape mathematical modeling of consumer and producer behavior in the private economy. Mathematical modeling not only made the presentation of economic principles easier to follow, but also gave the discipline the scientific image that the discipline aspired to achieve.

Although it is doubtful that many students of economics, at least in introductory classes, know of Walras's contributions, they are undoubtedly aware that the simultaneous determination of equilibrium in the goods and factors markets, and the notion of marginal utility have their origin in the works of Walras.

In short, the discipline of microeconomics, from its birth to its maturity, owes a debt to the thinkers of the seventeenth, eighteenth, and nineteenth centuries whose contributions made economics not only a worthwhile area of study but also a discipline worthy of the title of science.

If one looks beyond the origins of economic thoughts developed in the seventeenth, eighteenth, and nineteenth centuries and immerses oneself into the study of economics ideas developed in the twentieth century, one is struck by the fact that the discipline has morphed into something akin to pure science rather than social science. The use of mathematical symbols, equations, and graphs, as well as model testing, have transformed economics from an inquiry into the "Wealth of Nations" to a mathematical presentation of what constitutes the wealth of a nation and how to explain it, if not also to seek sources of augmentation of this wealth.

Critical to our modern understanding and teaching of economics is modeling and empirical testing. With this scientific transformation, students of economics are able to understand and appreciate how an economic system functions, its players, and their individual contributions to solving a complex host of societal issues.

With gains, there is always pain. Students of economics, especially at the graduate level, have to learn more than what they perhaps anticipated in their choice of economics as their field of study. What efforts they have put in, in terms of learning of other fields of study (mathematics, in particular), have their rewards. Not only have they been able to empirically verify or refute old theories and postulates, but most importantly they can also trace out the effectiveness of policies as they work through the economy.

Few dispute the contributions of mathematics and the scientific inquiry to our understanding of the economy and how policies put in place work out through the system. What needs to be said and emphasized is that these economic models are not fool proof. As Samuelson described it, the economist's model is not a controlled experiment in the lab. The economist does not deal with mortar and bricks; his subject of experimentation and modeling is fluid and often unpredictable "man". Yet there are common threads to all human actions to which economists hang on: choice, and maximization of self-interest, and in, not rare circumstances the "public" interest.

The micro foundations of the principles of the private economy owe a debt of gratitude to many economists of the twentieth century, most notably Paul Samuelson. Students of economics are indebted to his vast contributions to the study of microeconomics, his articulation through mathematical concepts of utility analyses, his theory of revealed preference, the derivation of welfare maxim, and the application of welfare economics to the study of public economics, to name a few. One has to look at the contents of two volumes: *The Collected Scientific Papers of Paul Samuelson*, volumes I and II edited by Stiglitz (1966) to appreciate how far the discipline has come and the contribution of mathematics to the economist's knowledge.

In one of his papers "The Empirical Implications of Utility Analysis," written in 1938 and reproduced in Stiglitz, Samuelson raises a fundamental question for micro analysis: "if the concept of utility has no empirical implications, then utility analysis is meaningless". Empiricism here would apply to price-quantity behavior.

Samuelson proceeded to show that the utility analysis in its "ordinal" form—more or less rather than the "cardinal" form requiring precise measurement—does indeed contain "empirically meaningful implications for the individual and group price and quantity implications" (Stiglitz, 1966, p.22).

Samuelson reformulation of utility in terms of revealed preference allows the economist to interpret choice not in terms of "unobservable" concept, that of utility, but through the observation of actual choice exercised by the individual and or the collectivity.

It would not be an exaggeration to conclude that two centuries later, the principles of the private economy laid down by the classical economists still remain as solid a foundation as when they were put forth in the eighteenth and nineteenth centuries. To be sure, new theories and models were formulated and empirically tested by the economists of the twentieth century, yet it is hard to envisage a structure no matter how grand without a solid and enduring foundation.

5   THE MACRO ECONOMY: THE WORLD OF JOHN MAYNARD KEYNES

"I believe myself to be writing a book on economic theory which will largely revolutionize not, I suppose at once, but in the course of the next ten years—the way the world thinks economic problems." (*Exerts from* a letter *written by Keynes* to George Bernard Shaw in 1935 *reported in Heilbroner, 1953*)

Keynes could not have been more right in assessing the contribution of his *The General Theory of Employment, Interest, and Money* (1936) to the discipline of economics, but most significantly to the changing character of political economy. Prior to Keynes's treatise the focus of political economists of the eighteenth and nineteenth centuries, especially those labeled as "classical economists," a phrase coined by Karl Marx, was on how a market system functions and the determination of factor returns.

As was discussed in chapter 4, considerable emphasis was placed by the classical economists on market structure (the assumption of a perfectly competitive market), on the determination of exchangeable value, the relationship between wages and profits, and the relationship between the money wage and necessaries of life. Unemployment when it existed was considered to be "voluntary" and self-correcting. Above all, the political economists from Smith, Mill, and Ricardo, to Marshall, along with others were of the view that a market economy, if left alone was capable of achieving full employment, "involuntary" unemployment cannot exist.

The classical teachings of the eighteenth and nineteenth centuries of these principles became known to students of economics as the study of microeconomics.

Macroeconomics, a term that emerged in conjunction with the Keynesian treatise on unemployment, interest, and money, unlike the classical theories, focuses on economic aggregates, that is, on how the "macro" economy functions. It deals mainly with the problems of unemployment and inflation.

To fully appreciate the contribution of Keynes's *General Theory*, not only to the subject of economics but also to the formulation of public policy, a brief background of events leading to the publication of *The General Theory* may be in order. Next, the foundation of *The General Theory* as put forth by Keynes is summarized.

The General Theory elicited a barrage of criticism from Keynes's peers, in particular from the American economists, including Paul Samuelson, Alan Meltzer, Gottfried Haberler, and Wassily Leontief. A sample of such a critique can be found in Seymour Harris's volume entitled *The New Economics* and published in 1952. Such critiques are enlightening in that they give students of economics as well as general readers of economics a taste of how an idea (or ideas) once born, takes on a shape that may or may not conform to the writer's original intent.

The Birth of the General Theory: A Brief Background

There are two names of economists that every student of economics and just about every politician of today and yesterday have heard of: Adam Smith, *An Inquiry into the Wealth of Nation* (1776) and John Maynard Keynes, *The General Theory of Employment, Interest, and Money* (1935).

For students of economics and the general public, at least those of the 1930s vintage and/or of the Nixonian era, the name of Keynes evokes many sentiments. As a depression economist, he saw no other way to rid the country (the American economy) of its massive unemployment than through a "visible" hand of government; or as an activist economist whose prescriptions were but evidence of socialist design.

The General Theory was published in 1936. Until the 1930s, the prevailing view, due mainly to the classical economists' doctrines, was that the economy is self-adjusting; that involuntary unemployment cannot exist. The Great Depression of 1929 changed this thinking.

Everyone knew, or at least has heard of the collapse of the stock market in the last week of October 1929. Within two months, the market lost some $40 billion of value, but the most fearful aspects of the depression were the fall of national income from $87 billion in 1930 to $39 billion in 1933, business investment had fallen by 94 percent. Worst of all was the fate of workers; the unemployment rate had reached record levels of 15 to 20 percent. The depression dragged on; the economy did not adjust to return to full employment the way the classical economists have presupposed.

The Great Depression may be said to have given credence to the name ascribed to Keynes' *General Theory* as "The Keynesian Revolution," for undoubtedly it has revolutionized thinking about how an economy functions. It offered four key postulates:

- The economic system is capable of remaining in a "chronic" condition of sub-normal activity for a considerable period (p.249).
- Full or even approximately full employment is of rare and short-lived occurrence (p.105).
- Consumption is the sole end object of all economic activities (p.104).
- New capital investment can only take place if future consumption is expected to increase (p.105).

These four postulates constituted what had become known as the "gloomy" diagnosis of *The General Theory*. The problem was simple: a lack of sufficient business investment; the solution put forth was equally simple: if businesses could not increase investment, someone else, i.e. the government, has to do it, and if this is not feasible, the government should aim at increasing consumption.

As we mentioned earlier, many in the business community thought of Keynes as advocating socialist policy that poses a threat to free enterprise. Keynes, however, emphasized in his treatise that he thought of the government as offering a helping hand, that it would concern itself only with providing enough investment, while leaving the works of the bulk of the economy to private initiatives (p.260).

Postulates of The General Theory

Keynes began his treatise by unraveling some of the postulates held by the classical economists. He criticized classical economists for failing to provide an adequate theory of what determines the actual employment of available resources. According to Keynes, the classical theory of employment was based on two fundamental postulates:

- That the average wage paid to labor is equal to the marginal productivity of labor.
- That the utility of the wage received by labor, when a given amount of labor was employed, was equal to the marginal disutility of that amount of employment (see Marshall's Postulates in the previous chapter).

The first postulate made by the classical economists defines the demand for labor schedule, the second the supply of labor schedule. These postulates, according to Keynes, did not allow for the possibility of involuntary unemployment (p.4).

That involuntary unemployment in the classical economists' world did not exist, except perhaps temporarily, was in essence the one postulate that gave rise to the revolutionary view of how a macro economy functions and for a proposal addressing the shortcomings of its functioning. In the first chapter of his *General Theory*, Keynes stated:

> "I shall argue that the postulates of the Classical Theory are applicable to a special case only and not to the general case—Moreover, the characteristics of the special case assumed by the classical theory happen not to be those of the economic society we actually live, with the result that

its teaching is misleading and disastrous if we attempt to apply to the facts of experience" (p.3).

From the classical economists' postulates, for income and employment to increase, one of two things has to happen: a reduction in the disutility of labor (work) or an increase in the marginal productivity. Keynes did not see how either of these conditions could be met, in view of the fact that the classical economists have maintained that the demand for labor may be satisfied before everyone who wants to work at the prevailing money wage rate is employed; and secondly, labor as a group may not want to work for less (see Marshall exposition in chapter 4).

Keynes also took issue with the premise that while workers may resist a reduction in money wages, it is unlikely that labor will withhold their labor, whenever there is a rise in the price of wage goods (necessaries).

Having disposed of the classical postulates as inadequate to support their contention that involuntary unemployment does not exist, Keynes set about to put forth his own theory of employment, offering two postulates and two definitions:

- The level of employment, both in an individual firm and in the aggregate depend on the amount of proceeds that the entrepreneurs expect to receive from the output produced.
- The proceeds that entrepreneurs expect to receive from the employment of a given amount of labor is defined as "the aggregate demand function".
- The aggregate supply price of output from employing a certain amount of labor is defined as the "aggregate supply function" and,
- The volume of output is given by the "equality" of the aggregate supply function and the aggregate demand function (p.25).

The value of output at the intersection of the aggregate supply function and the aggregate demand function is called the effective demand as at this level the entrepreneur expectation of profits is maximized. The insufficiency of effective demand will bring the increase in employment to a halt before full employment is achieved (p.31).

The insufficiency of aggregate demand is the obstacle that *The General Theory* aimed to address, not only to show how it comes about but also what can be done about it. Taking an example from history, Keynes stated, "Ancient Egypt was doubly fortunate and doubtless owed to this its fabled wealth, in that it possessed two activities, namely pyramid-building as well as the search for the precious metals, the fruits of which, since they could not serve the needs of man by being consumed, did not stale with abundance" (p.131).

That the level of output is determined by the equality of demand and supply is totally in contrast with the classical economists' (namely J. B. Say) ideas, which state that supply creates its own demand. Below we provide a brief sketch of Keynes's theory of employment.

The sequence of events that shape the employment outcome is spelled out as follows:

When employment increases, aggregate real income increases. The psychology of the community is such that when aggregate real income rises, aggregate consumption also rises but by less than the rise in real income. Keynes called this psychology the propensity to consume. Thus, it follows that the propensity to consume out of real income is less than unity.

The next logical step was to state the obvious: If an increase in aggregate real income does not raise consumption by the same amount, aggregate output cannot be sold; the level of employment cannot be maintained. Keynes offered the solution: To maintain a given level of employment, there must be an amount of investment sufficient to absorb the excess of total real output over what the community chooses to consume (p.28). From this the following propositions may be derived:

- The "equilibrium" level of employment, given the community propensity to consume, will depend on the amount of current investment.
- The amount of current investment depends on the inducement to invest.

- The inducement to invest will depend on the relation between two schedules; the marginal efficiency of capital schedule, and a complex of rates of interest on loans of various maturities and risks (p.28). This proposition is the basis of the Keynesian theory of interest and money.

Thus the basic ingredients in *The General Theory* are the propensity to consume, the marginal efficiency of capital, and the rate of interest. These three concepts were to be explored further in the *General Theory* (Book III and Book IV).

From these propositions, it follows that there will be one level of employment that is consistent with equilibrium—equilibrium is defined at that level at which there will be no inducement to expand or contract employment.

Keynes left a lasting imprint on the discipline of economics as he went about explaining how each one of these three elements—the propensity to consume, the marginal efficiency of capital, and the rate of interest—are determined, and the way the three elements interact with one another to exert a determinate effect on the level of real income and employment. In the analyses, Keynes injects another element: expectation.

In introducing expectation, Keynes's analysis may be said to be dynamic in that it has introduced time as an explicit factor in the determination of the level of economic activity, most significantly perhaps in the determination of the level of investment.

Time affects both the planning and execution of economic activities. According to Keynes, time usually elapses between the incurring of the costs of production and the purchase (sale) of the output (p.46). Because of this time lag, the entrepreneur has to form expectations about the future path of both the cost and the demand for the final product. These expectations are of two types: short-term and long-term expectations. Short-term expectations are concerned with the price the manufacturer expects to receive from selling the finished good; long term expectations refer to expectations about future returns the entrepreneur expects to earn on his investment associated with addition to his capital.

Of interest is the link Keynes postulated between short-term and long-term expectations. Short-term expectations are formed on the basis of the long-term expectations; hence, every decision the entrepreneur makes will depend on both the current or short-term as well as long-term expectations. The impact of expectations on the entrepreneur decision is clear. A change in expectation will affect employment and output. However, the full effect will only be realized over time. It follows then that "every state of expectations has its definite corresponding level of long period employment" (p.48).

The General Theory by all accounts has introduced new concepts and a framework of analyses that departed significantly from the classical economists' doctrine. Hence, Keynes needed (sometimes repetitively) to explain fully those concepts and to show how the parts fit into the whole.

The marginal propensity to consume is taken up in Book III, chapters 8, 9 and 10; the inducements to invest are discussed in Book IV, chapters 11 through 18. A digression from the main thesis—an analysis of money wages and prices (the domain of the classical theory)—is given in Book V.

The Marginal Propensity to Consume

Of the three concepts enumerated by Keynes, the marginal propensity to consume is perhaps the most familiar to students of economics. Admirers and critics alike agree that the marginal propensity to consume is at the heart of the Keynesian theory. The psychological law postulated by Keynes stipulates that when the real income of the community increases (or decreases), its consumption increases (or decreases), by less than the rise (or fall) in income. The relation was symbolically postulated to be less than unity (MPC < 1). From this Keynes offered the following hypotheses:

- If marginal propensity to consume is close to unity, small fluctuations in investment will lead to wide fluctuations in employment.
- If the marginal propensity to consume is low (close to zero), small fluctuations in investment will give rise to small fluctuations in employment.

Another implication of the marginal propensity to consume for the functioning of the economy arises from the interplay of a factor designated by Keynes as the "multiplier". The multiplier tells us that "when there is an increment of aggregate investment, income will increase by an amount which is k times the increment of investment ($k = 1/(1\text{-}MPC)$). Hence, the greater the marginal propensity to consume, the larger is the multiplier and thus, the greater the fluctuation in employment resulting from a given change in investment" (p.115).

The Marginal Efficiency of Capital

A simple way to explain this concept is to think of an individual purchasing a capital asset. With this purchase he expects to receive a series of returns from the asset over its lifetime. Hence, there is a relation between these expectations of yields and the cost or the purchase price of the asset. The rate of discount that the individual uses to apply to future earnings is what Keynes referred to as the marginal efficiency of capital (MEC). Formally, "The marginal efficiency of capital is the rate of discount which would make the present value of the series of returns expected during the lifetime of the asset just equals the purchase price of the asset" (p.35).

From this statement, it follows that the actual rate of current investment will be extended up to the point where the marginal efficiency of capital (the rate of discount) is equal to the rate of interest (the rate of interest being the opportunity cost of tying one's funds).

It is worth emphasizing at this stage that the marginal efficiency of capital is not a point, but rather it is a schedule, since its value varies with the level of capital (investment) being undertaken. The schedule declines as more and more investment is forthcoming. This schedule is of fundamental importance because through which the expectation of future returns influences the present.

The next step in the formulation of *The General Theory* is the determination of the rate of interest. A rate-of-interest schedule and the marginal-efficiency-of-capital schedule form the basis for an analysis of the fluctuations in the level of real aggregate output and employment. This analysis is taken up below.

The Rate of Interest

The first point Keynes emphasized is that the marginal efficiency of capital thought of as a discount rate is different from the prevailing interest rate (p.163). Whereas the schedule of the marginal efficiency of capital governs the terms on which loanable funds are demanded for investment purposes, the rate of interest governs the terms on which funds are supplied.

Interest, then, may be thought of as the price at which the desire to hold wealth in the form of cash at the available quantity of cash. Since the interest rate is a price, then if it was to fall (the reward to holding cash falls), then the total amount of cash people want to hold will exceed the available supply. On the demand side, the desire to hold cash is called the liquidity preference; the supply of cash (the quantity of money) then determines the actual rate of interest.

The question that may be raised at this point is: Why would anyone want to hold cash balances when the interest rate is greater than zero? The answer is uncertainty—uncertainty about the future of interest rates. Since people's expectations differ—"bears" and "bulls"—individuals who believe that future interest rates are likely to be above the rates assumed by the market would have reason to hold cash. The market rate of interest will be determined at the point where the sales of the "bears" and the purchases of the "bulls" are equal.

Keynes spelled out what liquidity preference (holding cash) entails: holding cash for transaction purposes, precautionary reasons, and the speculative motive—betting about the future. The liquidity preference like the marginal efficiency of capital is a schedule and not a point. It relates the demand for money to the rate of interest.

In his analysis of the demand (liquidity preference) and supply (quantity) of money, Keynes once more threw a wrinkle that made adjustments to full employment untenable. The wrinkle is the so called "liquidity trap" (the hoarding of money)—an increase in the quantity of money will have but a small effect on the interest rate. If the interest rate does not fall, or does not fall sufficiently, investment will not expand, and aggregate demand and employment will not increase.

Having enumerated obstacles like a "fickle" and "highly unstable" marginal efficiency of capital, a "liquidity trap", then according to Keynes, "it should be clear to the reader that full employment will not be achieved (p.204).

Something more has to be said about the quantity of money, since it has implications for other economic variables besides the rate of interest. This is taken up in the last part of *The General Theory.*

The Quantity Theory of Money

According to Keynes, money is a "suitable devise for linking the present to the future". And, as long as "there exists any durable asset possessing the quality of money, we cannot get rid of money". This gives rise to the characteristic problems of money economy (p.294).

The quantity of money plays an important role in a monetary economy, not only because it impacts prices and money wages, but it also impacts the level of effective demand. Keynes, put forth the following postulates:

- When resources are unemployed, an increase in the quantity of money will have no effect on prices; employment will increase by the same proportion as the increase in effective demand brought about by the increase in the quantity of money.
- When full employment exists, an increase in the quantity of money will increase money wages and prices by the same proportion as the increase in the quantity of money.

Keynes enumerated conditions under which the correspondence between an increase of the quantity of money and changes in money wages, prices, and money do not hold, but for the most part, the effect of an increase in the quantity of money falls on the monetary variables (p.298). In short, the long-term relationship between the quantity of money and the national income depends largely on the liquidity preference of individuals in the economy.

Summary

Putting together all the ingredients that make up the foundations of the *General Theory* (not a simple task to be sure), his fundamental propositions can be stated as follows:

- The two dependent variables (those whose determination is the focus of the *General Theory*) are employment and the level of national income.
- The independent variables that influence the determination of the levels of the two dependent variables; employment and national income are the psychological propensity to consume; the psychological attitudes to liquidity (liquidity preference) and the psychological expectations of future yields for capital (the marginal efficiency of capital); and the quantity of money.

It is worth noting the implications of these postulates for economic policy, as all the independent variables, are based on the psychological attitudes of the population. When unemployment exists, *then* the policy maker's task is complicated by the fact that these attitudes may be slow to change, and hence the effect of policies aimed at increasing employment and national income may be slow in generating change.

Keynes concluded his treatise on employment, interest, and money with a comforting thought: "It is an outstanding characteristic of the economic system in which we live that, whilst it is subject to severe fluctuations in respect of output and employment, it is not violently unstable" (p.249).

The Keynesian theory, especially the philosophy of governmental actions to spur the economy during slumps, lost its luster during the 1970s and especially in the 1980s during the Reagan tenure in the White House. It is not surprising for such a turnaround from activist fiscal policy, one that calls for expanding the scope of the public economy through an increase in public spending, to a policy of what was referred to then as supply-side economics. Monetary policy that was almost forgotten was also advocated and rules to set the interest rates proposed and administered.

The policy shift did not arise out of nothing. It was a reflection of the state of macroeconomic theory, which was undergoing a total transformation, from a focus on the unemployment and output gaps, to analyses and modeling of the tradeoff between these two aggregates. In the process, the so-called "efficient" level of wages, inflation, unemployment, and aggregate output rates were derived from mathematical modeling of the aggregate economy and "optimal" levels of policy variables calculated. The use of simulation became rampant, with not a single model replacing the Keynesian model; there was not a single remedy to the twin problem of inflation and unemployment gaining acceptance. The economics profession had a field day in the application of econometrics to macroeconomic issues and in the simulation of a variety of policy options.

The development of the principles governing the macro economy in the post-Keynesian era sprung from two notable events: first, the development of macroeconomic data, thanks to the efforts of Kuznets and the Bureau of Economic Analyses and second, the development of a theory of economic growth put forth by Robert Solow. Compiling data on national income (the National Income Accounts), made it possible to map the economy in terms of aggregate magnitudes and to relate the individual components of the accounts to the aggregate economy. Almost every macroeconomic text began with the national income accounts, which made it easy to proceed from the system of accounts to explain magnitudes such as private consumption, investment, government spending, and the trade balance.

The data made it possible to assign values to those Keynesian concepts such as the marginal propensity to consume or the government expenditure multiplier. Moreover, the data spurred the development and estimation of macroeconomic models and the testing of alternative policy options. The flip side of this significant development is the proliferation of empirical modeling and testing of hypotheses, and therefore the departure of the discipline from its basic function, which called for explaining the fundamentals of the macro economy to an obsession with modeling and simulation of whatever hypothesis the macro economist wishes to advocate.

Solow's growth model (1956) moved the study of macroeconomics away from its concern with such phenomena as unemployment and the inflation rate, to an analysis of the sources of economic growth. Hence, the concerns of the macro economist shifted from its traditional preoccupation with unemployment, the inflation rate, the liquidity preference, or the choice of and effectiveness of government policy instruments to the analyses and development of growth models. In other words the focus shifted from the short run to the longer run.

Of interest in the post Keynesian development of macroeconomics is the dichotomy between fluctuations and economic growth, even though the behavior of short term variables such as consumption and investment are central to the understanding of the process of economic growth. In short, advances made in macroeconomics in the post-Keynesian era have moved the discipline away from simply setting principles of economics to an integration of economic theory with applied economics.

Today, there exist dozens of macroeconomic models, some of which deal with long run growth, others with economic fluctuations. A fundamental ingredient in the analyses, whether the model deals with fluctuations or economic growth, is grounding in mathematics. This, along with knowledge of empirical modeling and the micro foundations of economic analysis, makes it possible for students of economics not only to comprehend the latest advances in the study of economics, but also to contribute to the body of knowledge about the macro economy.

A final note: Unlike the study of microeconomic phenomenon, macroeconomic theory has yet to reach its zenith. The search is still on for another *General Theory*.

6 PRINCIPLES OF POLITICAL ECONOMY: THE PUBLIC ECONOMY

> "It is common usage to speak of the public economy as the national household or as the case may be the country household, city household, or generally the public household. The whole public economy is thereby given a name taken from one single section of the private economy."
>
> —Friedrich Von Weiser, *A Theory of the Public Economy* (1924, p292)

The Public Economy

The foundation for the study of the public economy was laid out as early as the 1800s through the contribution of Adam Smith, David Ricardo, John Stuart Mill, and Leon Walras. Below we begin with a brief overview of this foundation.

Adam Smith, in his *Inquiry into the Wealth of Nations* (1776), dealt with the role of government, sources of revenues, and the public debt. These are, more or less, the domains of what is known today as public economics. The fact that Smith devoted 245 pages, or one quarter of the volume, to the public sector should not come as a surprise to readers, given his definition of the subject of economics reproduced earlier in chapter 2 of this volume. The definition Smith gave may surprise many in that not only did he consider political economy as a branch of the science of a statesman or a legislator, but also that one of its objectives is to supply the state with revenue sufficient for the public services.

This definition did not go down well with Walras. In his book, *Elements of Pure Economics* (1873), Walras launched a critique of Smith's designation of what political economy is about, but more importantly he was against Smith's lack of specificity about the two sides of the equation—the revenues and the expenditures sides of the budget. According to Walras, Adam Smith should have stressed first that "the aim of the political economy is to set forth the conditions for the production of a plentiful societal income, and second the conditions for an equitable division of this income between individuals and the State" (Walras, 1954 Ed, p.52).

Walras's critique was a bit harsh in that Smith was not concerned with the distribution of social income, but with the efficiency of production. Smith did enumerate bases on which taxes would be levied to defray government expenses, although not in conjunction with the provision of those services.

A second contribution to the study of the public economy is found in David Ricardo's *Principles of Political Economy and Taxation*. Ricardo devoted eleven chapters (100 pages out of 447) to the analysis of taxation. In those chapters, he dealt with the taxation imposed on different tax bases such as rent, land, gold, wages, profits, and so on, and he showed how the "incidence" of these taxes differed due to the shifting possibilities of the tax. Thus, Ricardo established principles for tax policy by analyzing the ultimate impact of each type of tax on the tax base. As to state services, Ricardo paid little attention to the role of the state in the provision of these services.

John Stuart Mill in *The Principles of Political Economy* questioned the prevailing wisdom about the functions that the state ought to perform, arguing that the role of government should not be a general one, but rather specific to the country and the time. Mill (Book V, Chapters I-VIII) explored both the type and scope of activities that should be carried out by the state. Mill, however, was of two minds about the functions that ought to be carried out by the state. He comes across as opposing the interference of government in the affairs of the individual, yet he also believed that certain functions needed to be performed by the state. A few quotations illustrate

Mill's difficulty in aligning himself with one side of the argument or the other:

> It may be said generally, that anything which is desirable should be done for the general interest of mankind or of future generations, but which is not of a nature to remunerate individuals for undertaking it, is a suitable thing to be undertaken by government. There are some things with which governments ought not to meddle, and others things with which they ought (p.885). As a general rule, the business of life is better performed when those who have an immediate interest in it are left to take their own course, uncontrolled either by the mandate of the law or by meddling of any public functionary (p.952).

On reflection, it is clear that Mill did indeed acknowledge the necessary presence of some form of authority, government, to address issues that are beneficial to individual members of the common. For example, by arguing that those matters of importance to future generations and those services that are of benefit to the community as a whole and not to specific individuals are to be provided by the state, Mill had indeed laid the foundation of what has become known in modern public economics as the theory of public goods. As we will discuss below, public goods are goods to be provided by the state, and whose benefits accrue to all.

On the other hand, one can see clearly the influence of Adam Smith's notion that the individual left alone will achieve the highest level of satisfaction and that the government should get out of his way. Still, Mill, as the next quotation suggests, was not totally convinced. He believed in equity in the distribution of income and wealth and went as far as developing a theory of redistribution of said income and wealth. Clearly for this task to be achieved, society would need a very "visible hand" of government. "One of the most unfeeling effects is a general increase both of production and accumulation. Industry and frugality cannot exist where there is not preponderant probability that those who labour and spare will be permitted to benefit" (p.697).

In effect early on in his volume, Mill devoted Book II to the issue of distribution of society's wealth. He argued that society cannot remain passive about the distribution of wealth. According to Mill, society can subject the distribution of wealth to whatever rules it thinks best, but who is likely to perform such a function. As he put it: it is up to the law and customs of society (p.201). Once again, the distribution of society resources appears in modern public economics as a function ascribed to the State.

Walras stressed the notion that an economy cannot function without the intervention of an authority to maintain order and security, to render justice, to guarantee national defense, and to perform many other services. Thus, essentially Walras highlighted all those functions identified by Smith, then set forth the principles that ought to govern the design of taxation.

Modern public economics did not resolve completely the issue classical economists struggled to resolve—the role of the state.

Paul Samuelson, a Nobel laureate in economics, made a valiant attempt at putting his views on this issue before students of economics. In three essays, "The Pure Theory of Public Expenditure" (1954), "Diagrammatic Exposition of a Theory of Public Expenditure" (1955), and "Aspects of Public Expenditure Theories" (1955). In his article "The Economic Role of Private Activity" reprinted in *The Collected Scientific Papers of Samuelson*, edited by Stiglitz (1966), Samuelson took on the task of airing the difficulties encountered in defining the role of government in a "free," market-oriented economy. He believed that the most effective way to highlight such difficulty was to put forth those definitions that were made by notable statesmen as well as notable economists. For a start, he posits the following:

"One way of approaching the question: What is the proper role of government is to ask, what is the proper role of nongovernment?" An answer to the second question would also provide an answer to the first (Stiglitz, 1966, p.1420).

Samuelson, showed that these two questions do not take us very far, for if we could define a nongovernmental role, let us say do nothing, this does not give us an answer, as there would be no need to ask the first question. Next, Samuelson reproduced few quotations (given below to shed light on the issue (pp.1421-1423).

It is worth noting that the quotations below reflect, according to Samuelson, American President Abraham Lincoln's view about the role of government, "I believe the government should do only that which private citizens cannot do for themselves, or which they cannot do well for themselves." Samuelson also quoted Thomas Jefferson as saying that the "government is best which governs least". Another quotation, attributed to distinguished economist Colin Clark, states that "the role of government must be held below a ceiling of 25 percent of the national income" (*The Collected Scientific Papers of Samuelson*).

Samuelson offered his own law about the role of government: "There are no rules concerning the role of government that can be established by a *priori* reasoning" (1966, p.1423).

Having highlighted the difficulties involved in providing a definition of the role of government that reasonable people might agree on, Samuelson proceeded to outline both graphically and with the aid of mathematics, a model explaining the optimal determination of government expenditures.

In putting forth his theory "The Pure Theory of Public Expenditures," he reminded his readers that the classical economists, Smith, Ricardo, and Mill, among others have neglected the study of public expenditures.

He cites a study by Pigou *A Study in Public Finance* (1965), a book of 285 pages where he gave most attention to taxation while devoting "barely half a dozen pages to expenditures". Samuelson acknowledged Sax, Wicksell, Lindhal, and Musgrave as the few economists, who did not neglect the theory of public expenditure.

Our journey through history of economic thought lead us to Smith, Ricardo, and Mill as they considered the role of government, which was followed by a review of contributions made by the twentieth-century economists, namely Musgrave and Samuelson to the study of the public economy.

As Samuelson pointed out earlier with reference to Pigou's volume, the classical economists have devoted most of their efforts to the study of taxation. As will be presented below, the principles of taxation put forth by the political economists of the eighteenth and nineteenth century have stood the test of time. That the modern analysis of taxation does not depart much from Ricardo's and Mill's theories, although it does add a great deal of sophistication to the exposition by modeling taxation within a given structure—the household, and/or the firm, utilizing the modern analytical techniques of macroeconomic modeling. The impact of this analysis put the principles of the public economy on par with the principles of the private economy, thus making it possible the integration of the public sector with the private sector in the study of economics. This integration was needed to evaluate the effects of tax policies on the aggregate economy, as well as on individual sectors of the economy.

As is the case with the private economy, a study of the public economy is not complete without addressing the whole range of activities that have taken place in the economy. By focusing only on the tax side of the public economy, with little if any attention paid to the expenditure side of the state budget, gaps of knowledge needed to be filled in order to provide a comprehensive theory of the public economy. This lack was addressed back in the 1950s by Samuelson and Musgrave. As will be shown below, a different view of the public economy is put forth by Nobel laureate James Buchanan and Gordon Tullock in their seminal work, *The Calculus of Consent* (1965).

The chronology of contributors to the principles of the public economy presented in this chapter begins with Adam Smith and concludes with James Buchanan and Gordon Tullock. Our task involved the distilling of the literature to uncover the principles that define the role and function of the public economy. We begin first with a definition of the public economy, which is followed by the principles of a public economy. There, we summarize the principles of taxation put forth by the classical economists Smith, Ricardo, Mill, and Walras. This presentation will be followed by Musgrave's views on the modern approach to tax theories.

An analysis of state expenditures—the theory of public expenditures—will be presented next. The last section is devoted to an overview of Buchanan's and Tullock's theory of collective action and the political economy of decision making.

Defining the Public Economy

The public economy may be defined by its players—the individual and the state—or it may be defined in terms of the functions that the state performs.

Analogous to the private economy, one may think of a market as having two players: the individual and the state. In the private economy, the individual interacts with another individual in the marketplace in his capacity as a buyer or a supplier of a private good. The market serves to satisfy both activities and the market is in equilibrium when neither the supplier nor the demander has the interest or inclination to change the outcome; equilibrium is reached when both parties are satisfied. In other words, no other solution is deemed an improvement over the one attained.

Under this definition, in the public economy, the players are the individual and the state. They come to the public market not on equal terms, as is the case in the private market. The state is an "unequal" partner in the public market. This inequality gave rise to economic doctrines aimed at explaining the interactions that take place between the individual and the state. This inequality, moreover, has led to the development of theories that have extended beyond the realm of economics to that of politics.

With regard to the second definition, the functions performed by the state depend on the "state" of the country. That is, in periods of war, the state acquires the needed resources without recourse to a market type transaction by commandeering or confiscating the resources needed to fund its war-related activities. In peaceful times, the scope of state's activities depends on the state's own view about its role and the reactions of the citizen. As will be discussed later on, in modern times, the state of the economy, unemployment, and/ or inflation has expanded the role of the state from a passive to an active player in the economy.

A distinguished feature of the public economy is the state's "sovereign" position over the life of the citizen. This sovereignty gives the state the freedom to define its objectives and provide it with the power to acquire needed resources. The only check on the state's sovereignty is the constitutional framework within which the state operates. In a democratic society, the constitution outlines the role of the state or sets up limits of its influence over the lives of individuals. In non-democratic states, there are few, if any laws that define the reach or the power of the state over the citizen. Modern public economics, the public choice school in particular, has had a profound impact on the principles of the public economy by addressing the framework within which the state and the individual interact through a democratic process.

In carrying out its activities, even in the state of limited government, the state acquires needed resources from its citizens. As Walras put it, there are only two ways the state can fund its activities: either "by holding property of its own," or by levying taxes on the incomes of individuals (1954 Ed, p.447).

With respect to the outcomes, the analogy between the private and the public economy breaks down. "The State is not a seller of its services" on the market on the principles of competition (price equals marginal cost) or monopoly (in pursuit of maximum net receipts). Rather, it often sells its services at a loss and sometimes gives them away without charge (p.449).

Unlike individuals acting as buyers in the private market place, the goods supplied by the state are "collective" goods. This aspect of the public economy gave rise to the principles governing the provision of collective goods as well as the determination of the "equilibrium" in their provision.

It is worth emphasizing again that almost all of the principles governing the raising of revenues to provide for the needs of the state have been laid out in the eighteenth and nineteenth centuries. On the other hand, principles of public spending were not fully explored or integrated in the study of public economics until the twentieth century. The foundation for a theory of public economics was laid out by Richard Musgrave, and Paul Samuelson. James Buchanan and Gordon Tullock provide a theory of the political economy of the public sector.[1]

The contributions of Buchanan and Tullock along with their predecessors (Duncan Black, Kenneth Arrow, Anthony Downs, and

---

[1] References to contributors to the theory of the public economy presented here is limited to the authors identified in the introduction to this volume.

Mancur Olson) are evident from their application of economics to the study of politics. As will be discussed later on in the chapter, the path-breaking contributions of Buchanan and Tullock in their book *The Calculus of Consent* (1962) led to a shift in the study of the public sector behavior and activities from the purely economic focus to the political framework within which individuals and the state operate—constitutional rules. The questions raised by the constitutional perspective involve the inquiry into the set of rules that "rational" individuals collectively agree on to ensure that they will be better off after the government is established than they would be in its absence.

Principles of Taxation

"Taxation under every form presents but a choice of evils; if it did not act on profit, or other sources of income, it must act on expenditure" (Ricardo, 1952 Ed, p.167).

The modern notion that taxes are the price that individuals must pay for the provision of public goods originated much earlier especially in the writings of Adam Smith and David Ricardo. Smith enumerated, in chapter II of his *Wealth of Nations*, the services that the sovereign is called upon to perform: defense, justice, public institutions, and public works. As these functions had to be financed through taxation, Smith set forth the principles that should govern the design of a system of taxation.

Tax Bases: Income or Expenditure

The first line of inquiry is to identify the sources from which revenues are to be obtained. Once identified, the principles that govern the allocation of tax shares will have to be specified. Smith identified three tax sources: those that are spelled out in the Constitution, funds belonging to the government, and funds from the people. Unlike the first two sources, taxes are levied on people's income, output, or assets. Therefore, principles had to be set forth to insure the application of the tax to the intended base and secondly, to determine the effect of the tax on the base (incidence). With respect to income, the base is rent, profits, and wages.

From Smith's exposition of the subject, the following tax principles may be stated:

- An income tax levied on the income base, could be limited to one base or applied to all bases.
- Tax contributions (tax shares) should be in proportion to ability to pay (this constitutes one variant of the ability to pay principle).
- The ultimate impact of the tax imposed on the tax base "is necessarily unequal" if it had no general effect on all bases. (This principle determines the incidence of taxation. Tax incidence depends on tax shifting).
- A tax on the wages of labor is "fully shifted" to consumers or landlords.
- A tax on the necessaries of life is equivalent to a direct tax on the wage of labor.

(This is the principle of equivalence of taxes.)

- The design of a tax (or a tax system) should consider, in terms of time and the manner of its application, the convenience of the taxpayer. This is the principle of minimization of the private cost of compliance.
- Administration of taxes should aim at minimizing the cost of collection. This is the principle of tax administration.
- Taxation according to ability to pay is easier to implement by indirect taxation (on expenditures) than by direct taxation (on income). This principle makes the case for the expenditure tax over the income tax.

David Ricardo: Principles of Tax Shifting and Incidence

Extensions and refinement of the principles of taxation posited by Smith are found in Ricardo's analysis of taxes. Ricardo devoted the bulk of his essays on taxation to the analysis of taxes imposed on returns (income) derived from economic activities. These included the taxation of rent, profits, and wages, as well as taxation levied on stocks, such as gold, houses, and land. Taxation levied on commodity was also analyzed by Ricardo, thus complementing his analysis of direct taxation (taxes on returns or incomes of the factors of production) with an analysis of indirect taxation (tax on commodities).

Ricardo's analysis of taxation was quite extensive. It ran the gamut from tax incidence to tax avoidance. The focus of Ricardo's study as distinguished from Smith's, lies in his interest in identifying the effects of taxation on the stock of capital, the transfer of capital assets, as well as the effect of taxation on the returns to the factors of production.

In some sense, Ricardo's analyses of taxation may be considered the forerunner of modern analyses of the taxation of income from capital and their allocative effect on society's use of capital (see, Arnold Harberger and Martin Bailey (1969)). According to Ricardo, "There are no taxes which have not a tendency to lessen the power to accumulate. All taxes must either fall on capital or revenue" (Ricardo, 1952 Ed, p.152).

From Ricardo's extensive analyses of the taxation of the incomes of the factors of production, the following principles may be stated:

- All taxes adversely affect capital accumulation.
- Taxes on the sales of land cannot be shifted. It falls on the returns to land.
- A tax on raw produce is shifted to consumers of the produce. It will have no effect on the quantity; it only has a price effect.
- A tax which raises the price of raw produce would raise the price of all commodities on which raw produce enters.
- Taxes on the transfer of property by sale or inheritance would be paid by the person receiving the property (the point of impact and ultimate impact are one and the same, no shifting).

The above five principles constitute the principles of shifting and incidence of taxation. Other principles formulated are tax avoidance where taxes on expenditures may be avoided, whereas taxes on returns to capital (profits) cannot; and that taxes diminish the enjoyment of income (the income effect of taxation).

John S. Mill and Leon Walras on Tax Principles

The topic of tax shifting and incidence of taxation occupied other political economists of the nineteenth century. Ricardo, Mill, and Walras dealt with shifting and incidence of taxation, as well as the allocation of tax burden under direct and indirect forms of taxation.

John Stuart Mill (Book V, chapter II) began his analysis by questioning some of Smith's four rules of taxation: that taxes are raised to support government's functions; the certainty of taxes; that taxes should be in proportion to ability; and that the tax should be levied at the convenience of the taxpayer.

As the statement above indicates, Mill's exposition of any economic concept or principle usually begins by taking issue with Smith exposition of the issue at hand. Of note is the fact that this practice has also been followed to some degree by Ricardo, Walras as well as other classical economists.

Mill's critical assessment of Smith's ideas was leveled against his concept of ability to pay. According to Mill, Smith needed to explore further the concept of ability, as it is often misunderstood. If as Smith postulated the tax should be proportional to ability and if taxation according to ability means "equal sacrifice," then one needs to inquire whether equal sacrifice means that "each individual contributes the same percentage on his pecuniary means" (p.812). As will be shown below, Mill modified Smith's rule of equal sacrifice by devising his own rule.

Mill also took an issue with the notion (advanced by both Smith and Ricardo) that taxation should not fall on capital. Although recognizing that the amount of national capital is of great importance, the taxation of capital per se does not diminish capital accumulation; it does so only when the tax is excessive. However, Mill modified the analysis somewhat in suggesting that there exists no tax that will not, at least in part, be paid by capital. "There is no tax which is not partly paid from what would otherwise have been saved—all taxes therefore are in some sense partly paid by capital" (p.812). The underlying assumption here is that saving is subject to the tax and that saving is used for capital accumulation. Having thus cleared the deck, Mill put forth his own principles or rules of taxation. Of note is the fact that Mill's extensive analyses are difficult to do justice to in mere lines or few pages. Nonetheless an attempt is made here to give the core analyses of Mill's on tax principles.

Since both Smith and Ricardo prior to Mill had formulated several principles of taxation that Mill has also advocated, we shall confine ourselves to presenting those principles put forth by Mill that not only were novel, but have also stood the test of time.

Two elements defining Mill's contribution to the theory of taxation should be distinguished. The first has to do with the definition of "ability to pay," and hence the development of the concept of equity; the second has to do with the "incidence" and the economic effects of taxation. Mill presented an extensive comparison between direct and indirect taxation in terms of efficiency, ease of tax administration, and compliance.

Before putting forth Mill's principles of taxation, it is worthwhile to note some of the frustration a reader may likely encounter in reading Mill's exposition of topics in his *Principles of Economics* volume. There is a tendency for Mill to offer an argument (or a refutation of someone else's argument) that sounds plausible, but then he turns around and offer an equally convincing and plausible refutation of the argument put forth.

For example, in comparing direct versus indirect taxation, Mill states, "If all taxes are direct, taxation would be much more perceived . . . and there would be a security . . . for economy in the public expenditures" (p.860). The visibility of a direct tax as compared to an indirect tax (an excise, a custom or a general sales tax) is one of the hallmarks of modern tax policy in many countries including the United States. On the assumption that taxpayers can ascertain with ease the tax falling on income (direct tax), as compared to a consumption or sales tax (indirect tax), it is argued that the burden of taxation felt under the income tax, because of its "visibility," will induce the taxpayers to assess the returns on their investment in the public sector. In other words, the visibility of the tax will induce the public to scrutinize not only the activities performed by the government, but also the utility at the margin derived from extending the size of government. This view is championed in the analysis of the optimum size of the public sector.

Having set forth the notion that direct taxes are more perceived than indirect taxes, Mill undermined somewhat this observation by stating that "although the argument is not without force, its weight is likely to be constantly diminishing . . . . The real incidence of indirect taxation is more generally understood" (p. 865). Having warned the reader about Mill's tendency to blur the issue, we turn now to his significant contributions to tax theory.

Mill on the Ability-to-Pay Principle

The general principle of taxation advocated by Mill is the ability to pay. To tax individuals according to ability, Mill explained that individuals with same ability, under this principle, should bear equal sacrifice. He defined this principle in terms of equity. Mill went on to state that the principle of equality of taxation, interpreted in its only just sense, equality of sacrifice, requires that a person who has no means of providing for old age, or for those in whom he is interested, except by saving from income, should have the tax remitted on all or part of his income which is really and *bond fida* (p.813). In the United States, the practice of allowing age and dependent exemptions to be deducted from income subject to the federal income tax goes partway in satisfying Mill's principle of equal sacrifice.

Equality of sacrifice would clearly require an assessment of individuals' circumstances. One way to circumvent this requirement is to exempt from the base a certain income that is used for a given purpose. There, Mill advocated the deduction of savings from income to arrive at the tax base. Accordingly "the proper mode of assessing an income tax would be to tax only the part of income devoted to expenditure, exempting that which is saved".

It is worth noting that Mill's definition of the income tax base as the part of income devoted to consumption was the basis for a tax theory advocated later on by Nicholas Kaldor (*An Expenditure Tax*, 1955) where he proposed replacing the income tax by an expenditure tax on grounds of equity as well as efficiency.

Mill stressed the fact that exempting savings from the income tax base, when invested, would give rise to tax liability on the income earned. Accordingly, the exemption of savings did not reduce the tax take, since the income received from investment would be subject to the tax.

Given that taxes can take the form of either direct taxation or indirect taxation, the principles governing the imposition of these two types of taxes needed to be spelled out and the outcomes contrasted.

Mill (Book V, III), provided a clear definition of what constitutes a direct tax: "A direct tax is one that is demanded from the very person who, it is intended or desired should pay it" (p.866). This is a general definition, as it accommodates both the taxation of income (income based tax) and expenditures (expenditure based tax). The important element here is that the tax cannot be shifted. An indirect tax on the other hand, is one that is demanded from one person but paid for by another. Excise taxes and custom duties are such taxes; hence the tax burden is shifted.

Having defined the two types of taxation, Mill proceeded to evaluate them based on three principles: tax incidence, convenience, and administration. Mill proposed the following rules for indirect taxation:

- The tax should be limited to luxury goods.
- The tax should not be demanded from the producer, but directly from the consumer (excise tax).
- The tax should apply to few goods. This rule would reduce the cost of collection.
- The tax should be levied on imported articles (customs duties are less objectionable than excise).
- The tax should not be sufficiently high to give rise to tax evasion.

Having established the principles of direct and indirect taxation, Mill provided some insight into how one might come down in favor of one or the other. The pros and cons he explored did not ultimately favor one type of taxation over the other; both direct and indirect can be avoided, and both taxes impose burden on taxpayers in that they reduce the level of consumption.

Next, Mill refuted the argument that indirect taxation was less "burdensome" than direct taxation, because "the contributor can escape the tax by ceasing to use the taxed commodity". Although the proposition is correct, Mill argued that there is a cost attached to this act; "he does so by a sacrifice of his own indulgence" (p.866).

Applying the tax principle advanced earlier, which calls for the tax to be imposed at the convenience of the taxpayer; indirect tax seems to win over the direct tax since the individual chooses the time and the manner in which the tax is paid.

To conclude his comparisons of the two systems of taxation, Mill argued that "direct taxes on income should be reserved as an extraordinary resource for great national emergencies" (p.866).

Walras on the Choice of the Tax Base, and Tax Incidence

Walras also addressed the choice of a tax scheme. First of all, he began by outlining ways in which the State can finance its expenditures. As relayed in chapter 2, Walras emphasized the fact that the state does not possess own resources to finance its services; its only option is "to make a levy on the income of individuals by taxation" (1954 Ed, p.447).

Walras put forth few principles of taxation. To derive these principles, he assumed first, that the economy consists of three classes of consumers: landowners, workers, and capitalists. The three classes correspond to the three factors of production, receiving the following incomes: rent, wages, and interest respectively. Second, that the state has the option of two types of taxation: indirect taxation and direct taxation. These two types are identified through their point of impact. This is determined by the method of collection: prior to the exchange or after the exchange.

Accordingly:

- A tax imposed prior to the exchange (point of impact) is an indirect tax; tax shifting will occur.
- A tax imposed after the exchange of services is a direct tax, it cannot be shifted.

Walras explained the shifting of the tax by arguing that if the state were to step in prior to the exchange by imposing the tax on the producer of consumer goods and services, the "entrepreneurs" clearly understood that they will reimburse themselves by adding the amount of the tax to the price. Hence a distinction is made between the two taxes: direct taxes are taxes on services, while indirect taxes are on products.

It is interesting to note the following proposition put forth by Walras: "When speaking of taxes, we are speaking of only the taxation of property and not of persons, for the latter sort of taxes cannot be assessed nor can their influence be traced" (p.450).

It may be of interest to put Walras's statement in a modern context. In the United States, especially during the discussion of the 1969 Tax Reform Act, the question was raised as to the appropriateness of calling the US Federal Income Tax the "individual," or the "personal" income tax. Those objecting to the use of those terms would likely have agreed with Walras that you can tax the returns to factors but not the factors themselves, except in the case of a head tax.

With respect to the taxation of the returns to factors of production, Walras stated the following principles:

- A direct tax on wages constitutes an act of appropriation by the state of a certain fraction of the worker wages.
- A direct tax on rent constitutes an act of appropriation by the state of certain fraction of the landlord's income and a corresponding fraction of the landed capital belonging to the landlord.
- A tax on land cannot be shifted to consumers of the landlord products.
- A proportional land tax will make the state a coproprietor of the land.
- A general tax on all interest charges to capital, all capitalists would be affected in proportion to their incomes; if the tax were imposed only on some but not all interest charges to capital, the tax would be equivalent to a consumption tax.
- A direct tax on all categories of interest charges encourages consumption and adversely affects capital formation.

As to tax shifting and incidence, Walras emphasized that a tax on commodities does not raise the price by the same amount of the tax, but rather it depends on the elasticity of supply and demand (Walras, p.458).

Walras's analysis of taxation as outlined above touches both on the taxation of fixed factors, such as land, as well as variable factors such as labor and capital. Walras modeled the effects of taxation on the returns to factors under both direct and indirect taxes. Although the analysis of incidence was put forth in mathematical form, Walras did not rely simply on the mathematical presentation to identify the tax incidence. He discusses such effects by presenting examples like the taxation of rent and wages to show the burden of the tax, that is, the final impact of the tax.

A feature of Walras's analysis that distinguishes it from those of others, like Ricardo or Mill is that Walras had more than once emphasized the notion that the tax falls on the returns to factors and not on the factor themselves, and that the state in imposing a tax on the returns to factors, especially fixed factors (land) does acquire some level of ownership of said factors. Moreover, the use of mathematical equations, especially in the analysis of tax incidence, although put in a simplified framework, has remained essentially the same today as it was then.

Modern Tax Theory

Having summarized the principles of taxation put forth by some political economists of the eighteenth and nineteenth centuries, we turn next to the modern version of tax theory. An exposition of the theory is contained in Richard Musgrave's volume *The Theory of Public Finance* (1959).

Richard Musgrave: Two Approaches to Taxation

Building on the contributions of his predecessors, and in light of the advances made in the branch of economics known as "welfare economics," a restatement and refinement of tax concepts and principles were put forth by modern economists; foremost amongst them is Richard Able Musgrave.

Musgrave broke down the historical development of the principles of taxation into two major approaches: the benefit approach and the ability to pay approach. Hence it became common when writing about tax theory to divide the subject in the two.

Two Approaches to Taxation

Tracing back the history of tax principles, we have shown in this chapter that both approaches to taxation have been touched upon by Smith, Mill, and Walras. Since that time many political economists have contributed to the study of tax theories culminating into the modern version of taxation—one theory advocates taxation according to benefits and the other according to ability to pay. We begin with the benefit principle or approach to taxation.

The Benefit Approach

Recall that Adam Smith in defining the subject of economics referred to it as a "branch of science of a statesman," and that one of its objective is "to provide the state with revenue for funding public services". This statement suggests that the end result of taxation is the provision of public services. These services were enumerated by Smith as follows: the protection of the nation, the protection of individuals, and the supply of goods and services that the individual or a small group of individuals cannot shoulder its expenses.

Although Smith's statement may be taken as the building block for a tax theory based on the benefit approach, it failed to tie in "benefit received" to the "tax levy". Put differently, the tie in between a benefit received and the tax paid requires an assessment of the tax levied in relation to benefit received. Musgrave in his volume was one of the early writers in the field of public economics to articulate such a link. He began his exposition with a comprehensive review of the early views and writings on the approach to benefit taxation. From Musgrave's historical review, one discerns a rise and a fall of the benefit taxation approach through time.

According to Musgrave's review, the principle of taxation which advocated that taxes should be based on benefits was put forth by political theorists of the seventeenth century. German writers held the view that the tax is the "price" of services rendered by the state. Subsequently, eighteenth century writers, including David Hume, subscribed to this theory.

The proposition upon which the benefit principle of taxation was laid was in a sense the "raison d'être" of its demise. By tying in taxation to a very narrow definition of benefits from public services—protection, the eighteenth century political theorists and their views led to the proposition that the tax levy should be limited to the financing of this service (Musgrave, p.68).

A revival of sorts took place at the end of the nineteenth century. Taxation according to benefits was advocated by several Italian writers including Pantalioni, Mazzola, and de Viti de Marco (see Musgrave and Peacock, eds., *Classics in the Theory of Public Finance*, 1958).

Major revisions to the benefit approach were made by other political economists of the twentieth century. It was argued that the benefit received is to be assessed by the individual receiving the benefit, thus making the tax share dependent on the subjective evaluation of the benefit. This fundamental change in the approach to taxation resulted in a theory of the "public household," i.e. government based on the "voluntary exchange principle" (Musgrave, 1959, p.69). The name most commonly associated with the voluntary exchange approach to tax theory is that of Erik Lindhal (1919). The underlying principle of the theory may be stated as follows:

- "Taxation should be just."

Application of this principle clearly requires a great deal of information about individuals' "subjective" valuation of public services as well as their willingness to reveal this valuation in a "quasi" market setting. Moreover, for the tax to be "justly" allocated, knowledge of pre-tax income distribution was needed.

Lindhal, in developing his model assumed that in pre-tax benefit-scheme income distribution was fair. Accordingly, the price paid for public services (the tax share) by each individual depends on the individual valuation of the benefit received. Lindhal's tax principle, then, results in differential prices or tax shares paid by individuals. Differential tax shares would satisfy the ability to pay principle. Musgrave took issue with this supposition, arguing that it cannot be taken as distributional corrective since Lindhal's model assumes a proper distribution of income to begin with (p.78).

The voluntary exchange theory as a basis for allocating tax shares according to benefits received, according to Musgrave, although intellectually appealing—especially for its approach to the equilibrium determination of the public budget—could not serve as a practical guide to tax policy. Thus, once more, ability to pay gained its prominence as the theory for tax policy.

The Ability to Pay Principle

This principle, as we saw earlier, was embraced by early writers, although it was perhaps best articulated by John Stuart Mill (see above discussion). Musgrave provides not only a restatement of the principles upon which the theory was based, but also augments the analysis by addressing three elements needed for a tax theory based on ability to pay. These are an index for measuring ability to pay, measurements of equal sacrifice, and a tax formula satisfying the concept of equal sacrifice.

With respect to the first element of the theory, determining an index for ability to pay, it is evident that "income," however defined, was chosen as the measure of ability. This is inferred from the application of this measure leading to the choice of personal income as the basis for taxation. The only sticky issue was that of determining income for tax purposes: whether, as Smith had argued, that it should be income above subsistence level, or according to Mill, it should be income minus saving. The modern application of this concept seems to favor Smith's notion over that of Mill. Most countries today, do allow for some level of exemption from income prior to the application of the tax to income.

The contribution made by Musgrave may be ascertained from his exposition of the concept of equal sacrifice. As discussed earlier, although Mill did advocate taxation according to this principle, he stopped short of providing a comprehensive definition of the term. Musgrave's analysis addresses this shortcoming.

Musgrave makes a distinction between three concepts: equality of absolute sacrifice, equality of proportional sacrifice, and equality of marginal sacrifice. In order to translate these concepts into tax principles, the utility derived from income (utility function) is needed. Accordingly, sacrifice was to be measured not by dollars and cents, but by the utility attached to those dollars and cents.

Based on the sacrifice theory, the following principles are derived:

- Taxes on income should be allocated among taxpayers in such a manner that the loss in utility associated with the loss in income is the same for all. This is the principle of equal, absolute sacrifice.
- Taxes on income should be allocated among taxpayers in such a manner as to equate the loss in utility in proportion to total utility for all taxpayers. This is the principle of equal proportional sacrifice.
- Taxes on income should be allocated among taxpayers in such a manner as to equate at the margin the loss in utility for all taxpayers. This is the principle of equal marginal sacrifice.

These principles can be translated into tax schedules under the first principle, equality of absolute sacrifice; the tax paid would be equal at different levels of income. The supposition, here, for translating the concept into a tax schedule, is the assumption of "constant utility" at different levels of income.

With respect to the equality of proportional sacrifice, the design of a tax schedule to satisfy this principle turned out to be a bit difficult. As Musgrave points out that the application of this principle requires an assumption about the shape of the utility schedules of individuals. If the marginal utility of income were constant, then this principle would call for proportional taxation, so that the taxes paid by individuals with different incomes give rise to proportional sacrifice, or a proportionate loss in utility.

The application of the principle that calls for the equality of marginal sacrifice also requires the determination of the shape of the utility schedules of individuals. If the assumption of declining marginal utility of income is accepted (which was established by Pareto, Jevons, and Walras), then the application of this principle would yield a progressive tax schedule on income.

The tax principles put forth under either approaches to taxation, the benefit approach, or the ability to pay approach have in large measure depended on developments in other areas of economic studies. As we saw earlier, translating a principle of sacrifice into a tax scheme required the knowledge of the shape of the income utility function of taxpayers. Moreover, the concept of equality or equity required an assessment or a measure of the "welfare loss" attributed to the loss of income due to the tax as well as the "welfare gain" associated with government expenditures.

Development in political economy, in particular the development of welfare rules put forth by Edgeworth and Pigou made it possible the translation of the equality of sacrifice principles into equity principles. Moreover, as will be presented in the next section on public sector's functions, equity as a principle for allocating the tax burden had to be viewed in conjunction with benefits received from public sector activities. Since both instruments of the public sector alter the distribution of society's income, the welfare principles applicable to the public sector in its capacity as a provider of services and as agent affecting the transfer of income from individuals to itself needed to be established. Pigou and Dalton set forth these principles to serve as guide for budget policy (Musgrave, p.113).

State Expenditures: From Smith to Musgrave

"It is of the highest importance, therefore to know distinctly what government cannot do as well as what it can do" (Malthus, 1969 Ed, p.522).

It is perhaps fitting that we start this section on the role of the state with a Malthus quotation, as it highlights once more the difficulty facing political economists of today as well as those of yesterday of coming up with a statement outlining the role of the state. Earlier, we provided quotations used by Samuelson to remind students of the public economy of the difficulties encountered in defining the role of the state, a definition that reasonable people, however one may define being reasonable, could agree on.

Today students of economics do not hesitate to enumerate for one and all, the role of the state as a provider of public goods, as well as other modern functions such as the stabilization of the private economy and the redistribution of social wealth. Yet, those who have studied Musgrave's *Theory of Public Finance* and the contributions of early writers, which are contained in the Classics, would undoubtedly state that we (economists) have yet to come to grips with what the government ought to do and what it ought not do.

Having acknowledged the problem of ascertaining what governments ought or ought not do in every time and space, an attempt will be made in this section to review the contributions of Paul Samuelson and Richard Musgrave in conjunction with what Smith and Mill stated about the role of government (see above) in order to stand back and see whether one can surmise with some clarity not what governments should do but what they should not do.

History dictates that we start with Smith. Recall that Smith in his *Inquiry of the Wealth of Nations* enumerated the expenses that would be needed to fulfill state's functions. These functions were identified as defense, justice, public works, and public institutions. Smith assigned the logic for ascribing these functions to the state, by arguing that these functions are not optional, but rather that it is the state's duty to perform them.

As Smith put it, "The first duty of the sovereign [is] that of protecting the society from the violence and invasion of other independent states . . . the second duty of the sovereign [is] that of protecting as far as possible every member of the society from injustice or oppression . . . the third and last duty of the sovereign is that of erecting and maintaining those public institutions and those public works" (Smith Book V, p.3).

The first two functions are more or less agreed upon by people independent of their political orientations: laissez faire or planning. The third function however, carries with it a burden of interpretation. The laissez-faire ideology would require a narrow definition of this function, whereas a planner would call for much wider interpretation, covering all those functions that a planned economic system would call for.

It is worth noting at this juncture that Smith was forceful in ascribing to the state more functions such as the education of "common" people (Book V, p.3), than what "laissez faire" advocates, who championed Smith notion of the "invisible hand" would acquiesce to.

Smith however did not lay out rules or principles that the "sovereign" ought to follow in satisfying these functions. Neither did he tie in the tax side of the sovereign budget to the expenditure side. The concept of a budget for the sovereign had yet to be developed at the time of the writing of Smith's *Inquiry*, and hence the focus was not on (what we study today) the optimal budget or the principles of budget allocation.

Nevertheless, as was discussed earlier, Smith spelled out, in great detail the sources of revenues and the principles that should govern the raising of these revenues, which would be needed to fund the three functions of the sovereign which he had enumerated. The two sources of revenues identified by Smith are general revenues and user charges.

A public spending principle, which one may arrive at from Smith's study of the role of the sovereign may be stated as an inquiry: whether the individual, left to pursue his own interest would better his own interest as well as the interest of the common.

Musgrave on the Role of Government

Students of public economics (formerly referred to as public finance) will ascribe to Richard Abel Musgrave the title of the father of public finance (see A.Ott (2008) "A Tribute to Richard Abel Musgrave"). As relayed earlier, there were no shortages of opinions about what the state or the sovereign ought or ought not to do. But these opinions and contributions of the political economists of past centuries fell short of providing a comprehensive blueprint for the role of the state and the principles that should govern its participation in a market-oriented economy. Moreover there were no attempts made to integrate both sides of the public budget, or as Walras might have put it, the two sides of the equation; that is to say there was no attempt made to tie in the function of raising revenues with the function of expenditures. No budget decisions were stated, and neither was the role of the individual taxpayer, who is called upon to shoulder the expense of the sovereign.

Richard Musgrave filled this void. His *Theory of Public Finance* offered students of the public economy a systematic way to analyze the functions of government, its tax and expenditure allocation, and the budget outcomes.

Musgrave's volume was clearly founded on the works of those who preceded him. But his contribution stands as a monumental achievement in its focus on the state as a unified body—a third player in an exchange economy. The first task in the analysis of the public sector is to highlight the difference between the private economy and the public economy.

The Market versus the State

In a private goods market, the private exchange of goods is the efficient mode, whereas in the public market, the exchange is a social exchange that may involve "externalities" that are not met by the private exchange. Externalities (this term refers to the external effect imposed by one individual action on another) require a political process to deal with them, hence the need for a public means to address them. A visible hand of government in this case is as natural phenomenon as is the invisible hand in the private market (Musgrave, 2008, p.49).

Musgrave views the state (henceforth referred to as the public sector), as the instrument by which the needs and concerns of the citizens are met. He views the public sector as a complement and not as a substitute to the private market.

To draw a clear distinction between the two types of exchanges—the private versus the public exchange—Musgrave provided a framework to describe the exchanges that take place between the state and individuals in the public economy. This framework is referred to as the three branch model.

The Three Branch Model

Perhaps the most famous, or more accurately known, feature of Musgrave's *Theory of Public Finance* is his "three branch model". Musgrave, developed the three branch model, not for the purpose of depicting the organization of the public sector, but to make the presentation of a complex task, a catalog of the sector's activities, better understood. According to Musgrave, the three branch model was needed in order to structure the whole of public finance into a common frame.

As he put it: "There is no simple set of principles, no uniform rule of normative behavior that may be applied to the conduct of the public economy. Rather, we are confronted with a number of separate though interrelated functions that require distinct solutions" (p.5).

To obtain a comprehensive, if highly simplified view of the problem, he presented the determination of budget policy in an imaginary state, where efficient standards of fiscal policy prevailed. The responsibility of the state's fiscal department was enumerated as follows: allocation (more accurately reallocation) of resources; distribution of income and wealth; and secure economic stability.

The three branches of the budget office would then be the allocation branch, the distribution branch, and the stabilization branch.

From the outset, Musgrave insisted that this separation is for the purpose of ease of presentation and should not be taken as representing separate branches of government performing separate functions without impacting the activities carried out by one branch or the other. Clearly, a change in the allocation of society resources would impact the distribution of real personal income as well as on the national income, which would require action to be taken either by the distribution branch and/or the stabilization branch of the government. In short, he needed to emphasize the nature of the exercise and that it was necessary to come up with a simple analytical framework of budget decisions, so that it may be possible to evaluate the outcome. The functions of the three branches are briefly sketched out below.

The Function of the Allocation Branch

A fundamental assumption for this function to be undertaken is an acknowledgment that certain types of goods or services cannot be provided by the private goods market. And, in addition, if the private goods market could supply them, the cost of provision of such goods is so high that it would not be feasible for one or few individuals to bear the cost. This proposition was maintained by both Smith and Mill (see above). Given the existence of these types of goods and services, the function of the allocation branch is to come up with an "optimal", best, scheme for reallocating society's resources, from private use to public use, in order to meet the cost of provision. The principle governing this reallocation is at the heart of a theory of public goods. The development of such a model using the logic of mathematics and through diagrammatic exposition is attributed to Samuelson. The model was somewhat simplified by Musgrave and used in the analysis of the allocation function of government in the three branch model.

The function of the distribution branch in Musgrave's three-branch model is to effect redistribution of income and wealth, if redistribution is deemed necessary. This is perhaps the most difficult and controversial function of government even when principles of equity are brought in the analysis to generate an acceptable criterion for redistribution. As will be presented below, this function is not an easy one to navigate no matter how articulate the theory that is put forth in favor of redistribution.

The function of the stabilization branch falls in the sphere of macromanaging the economy. It sprang out of Keynes' *General Theory*. As Keynes pointed out, a market economy will more often than not encounter episodes of involuntary unemployment and is prone to experience booms and busts (see chapter 5 in this volume). If one were to accept this prognosis, then a role is carved for the stabilization branch to implement those actions that restore full employment and economic stability.

The stabilization function of government did not stand the test of time. Advances made in the study of macroeconomic theory and monetary economics impacted the analyses of the stabilization function of the government, by relegating this function to monetary policy which in the United States is carried out by an independent agency; the monetary authority (the Federal Reserve). Accordingly, not much space will be given here to the function of the stabilization branch of Musgrave's the three branch model.

Having briefly described the three branch model, the state function that stands out among all three functions identified by Musgrave is clearly the reallocation function. In reallocating society resources from private use to public use, those principles that govern such reallocation need to be put forth and evaluated. As Smith put it before us, the reallocation of society resources should be based on certain requirements: that the goods provided by the state possess those characteristics that made it necessary for the state to undertake their provision (see above). Given the necessity that the public sector address these provision, principles need to be established to insure that the reallocation of private resources from the private economy to the public economy is carried out with minimum distortion. Moreover, in carrying out the provision of public sector goods, the standard of efficiency is applied.

Before setting forth these principles, we need first to identify those activities or goods the allocation branch is called upon to supply. Two types of provisions have been identified by Musgrave: "social" or collective wants and "merit" wants. We begin with a discussion of social wants.

Social Wants

According to Musgrave, the best way to describe these wants is by reference to private wants such as bread, cloth, and so forth. The nature of private wants is that these wants can be satisfied through the exchanges in the market place. A necessary requirement for such exchanges to take place is the existence of property titles for the things that are to be exchanged. For example, an exchange of money for bread requires that the individual has a property right over the good to be exchanged. The same is true in a barter economy with private goods in the exchange. Thus, in the private economy, the exchange principle is the mode of operation. This mechanism, however breakdown in the public economy in the case of social wants.

Social wants are "those wants satisfied by services that must be consumed in equal amount by all". As there is no requirement, like the private exchange, that consumption of the good entail payments, there is no such requirement in the case of social wants. In other words, those who do not pay are not excluded from the consumption of the social wants. This feature is called the "exclusion principle"; it applies to private good exchanges, but does not apply to the case of social wants (Musgrave, 1958, p.9). Examples of such social wants are protection from outside invasion (defense), police protection of persons and property, justice, and the like. The distinguishing characteristic of social wants is that they are available to all members of society without the requirement of payment—the exclusion principle does not apply—and that the consumption of one individual of the social want does not reduce the available amount for consumption to others (the consumption of every individual is equal to the total provision). Accordingly, the following principles may be stated:

- The satisfaction derived by any one individual from the provision of the social want is independent of his own contribution.
- Social wants must be satisfied through the public budget if they are to be provided at all.

This second principle is required as the cost of provision exceeds any one individual's ability or group of individuals' abilities for undertaking the provision.

The next issue Musgrave addressed is the determination of the level of provision. In the private economy demand and supply determine the level of provision of private goods. The demand for private good plays a critical role in that it reveals the preferences of consumers for private goods. In the public economy, there exists no such mechanism for preferences revelation for social wants. The questions that had to be addressed, then, are: first, what mechanism is there by which the government can determine the level of provision of social wants; and secondly, what social wants should be provided, given that resources are not unlimited; and thirdly, how can the cost of provision of social wants be spread among society's members.

The answers to these questions are not found by recourse to the private market. The state has to rely on a political market for answers to these questions.

In a democratic society, the decision rests with the political actors. The political process is substituted for the private market process. Individuals in this setting are called upon to adhere to the political (group) decision subject to the voting rule—majority, unanimity, or plurality. (The political process is taken up later on in the chapter in conjunction with the presentation of the Buchanan/Tullock theory of public choice).

The finance of social wants provision involves the imposition of taxes on individuals. How to distribute the cost (taxes) among individuals is subject to the evaluation that would be undertaken by the distribution branch (in Musgrave's three branch model) with regard to the proper or equitable distribution of income. The distribution of taxes could be progressive, regressive, or neutral, depending on the existing state of income distribution. If the prevailing distribution were one that met society's preferences, the distribution of the tax bill would likely be neutral in its effect on the distribution; it would not lead to a redistribution of private incomes. On the other hand, if the distribution of income did not meet with society's standards of equity, the distribution of the tax bill would not be neutral; a progressive taxation (or regressive) would be implemented.

The second category of wants discussed by Musgrave is merit wants.

Merit Wants

A great deal of difficulty and controversy has arisen in conjunction with Musgrave's notion of merit wants. The first question that was raised is what type of want or good that warrants the meritorious label? And, if a want or a good carried the label of a merit want what justification should there be for the public sector provision of this good? Most importantly, how should the cost of provision be allocated?

The first item, then, is to define the merit want. Musgrave defines merit wants as "wants that possess private goods characteristics, that they can be supplied in the private market, however what give them the 'merit' status, thus calling for public provision is the one characteristic that is so meritorious that society needs to insure their availability to citizen" (p.13). Merit wants refer to such items as school lunch programs, elementary and secondary education, vaccination programs, free or subsidized milk programs, free or subsidized health care clinics for the poor, and so forth. The meritorious aspect of education is that it gives rise to a more skilled population. Likewise, there are benefits that can be derived from good health. A healthy population is good for individuals' well-being as well as for the functioning of the private economy, as it reduces the loss of workdays and improves performance.

Unlike social wants, preferences for merit wants are not difficult to ascertain. The problem however is with the public sector's provision of merit wants in that such provision interferes with consumer preference. The example that is frequently cited is free but compulsory education. Education is viewed by many as a merit good; accordingly the state provides free compulsory education, at least at the elementary level. But, according to critics, despite its meritorious feature, this is a coercive act by the state and thus contributes to a loss of welfare.

Because of this aspect, the interference with consumer choice, the determination of the level of provision of merit wants, as well as the allocation of the cost of provision have to be made through the political process, where individuals' preferences may be expressed. However, to insure a level of provision, Musgrave advocated that majority rule be used to reach a decision.

The Distribution Branch

The distribution branch in Musgrave's three branch model is called upon to serve two functions: first, to insure that the distribution of income is in line with society's preferences, and second, to raise the necessary revenues that are needed to finance the provision of social and merit goods decided upon in the allocation branch.

If the private market outcome with regard to the distribution of private income corresponds to the preference of society, then the task of the distribution branch is reduced to raising and allocating necessary revenues to meet public goods provision. In doing so, the ensuing distribution of tax shares has to be neutral with respect to the prevailing income distribution. On the other hand, if the existing distribution differs from society's preferences then the tax allocation has to be set in such a way that the allocation of tax shares achieved the desired income distribution. Accordingly, the tax bill distribution may either be progressive or regressive as the case may be. Transfer payments may be used along with taxation to achieve the desired distribution.

Social philosophies or personal predilection with regard to equities or inequities differ. Yet within limits, there is likely to exist at any time and place more or less accepted mores with regards to certain basic aspects of the problem. In other words, there are some distributional issues that members of society are likely to agree on. For example, that babies would not go without milk or that a person in extreme poverty should be taken care of (Musgrave, p.18). Beyond these extreme cases, there is no easy way to deal with the problem of redistribution.

Under the assumption that there exists a preference for some redistribution of private income and wealth, then the function of the distribution branch is to devise a tax-transfer scheme that does not interfere with the optimal or efficient allocation of resources. The Samuelson "Pure Expenditure Model" described below provides the ingredients for such a mechanism.

The third branch of the budget in Musgrave's model is the stabilization branch. It operates under the assumption that both the allocation and distribution budgets satisfy their objectives. The remaining issue is for this branch to insure that the level of government taxes and expenditures is compatible with the twin objectives of full employment and economic stability. If the economy were at full employment—that is society's resources are fully employed—then the additional spending by the government would be inflationary, unless the spending were accompanied by tax increases sufficient to keep the private plus public spending compatible with price stability. In short, public spending on social and merit wants must be accompanied by a reduction of private spending, so that aggregate spending does not lead to inflation.

Likewise, in periods of unemployment, taxes imposed to fund the allocation branch expenditures, as well as those taxes that are needed to effect redistribution, have to be designed in such a way that the government tax program does not aggravate the slack in the economy. In short, the functions of the three branches of the budget not only have to be coordinated but also that the impact of their individual activities must be in sync with the private economy.

From the above discussion, it is evident that an analysis of the public sector's activities cannot be complete without addressing the efficiency issue arising from the transfer of private resources from private use to public use. The efficiency issue however requires modeling of the two sectors of the economy in a general equilibrium framework. The Samuelson theory of "Pure Public Expenditure" utilizes this framework to derive those efficiency conditions for the allocation of society's resources in order to satisfy the provision of both public goods (social and merit wants) and private goods, as well as the allocation of these goods among members of society.

Samuelson: The Theory of Public Expenditures

In three articles, published in 1954-55, Samuelson derived the efficiency conditions using the economist's framework of exposition, both diagrammatically and through the use of mathematical modeling. In its most simplistic form, the problem is cast in terms of two goods—the public good and the private good—and two individuals. A basic assumption of the model is that preferences of the two individuals are known, so that it is feasible to represent these preferences with the aid of a utility function or graphically in terms of indifference curves.

Obviously the preferences of the two individuals are assumed to differ; otherwise the model collapses to a one-person model. Moreover, if the assumption that the individuals' preferences for both types of good are known is dropped, then it is not possible to derive the efficiency conditions. In effect, Samuelson developed his model to solve the efficiency problem in the absence of a mechanism for preference revelation for public goods. He referred to the problem as one arising from "market failure". Since the market failed to reveal individuals' preferences for public goods, the government is called upon for their provision.

In his expenditures model, Samuelson explicitly integrates the activities of the two branches of the budget—the allocation branch, which provides public goods, and the distribution branch, which allocates tax shares, into his model in solving for both the efficient supply of both private and public goods and the assignment of tax shares to the two individuals. In the diagrammatic presentation of the model, Samuelson derives a production "possibility" curve that shows all the combinations of private and public goods the economy is able to deliver if all the resources are employed. Next, he derives, based on the preferences of the two individuals, the "utility frontier" reflecting the utility derived by the two individuals under different ways of sharing the two goods. From these two representations—the production possibility curve, or the production frontier and the utility frontier, the efficient solution to the allocation problem is arrived at.

Given that society was assumed to consist of two individuals whose preferences for the public good differ and that their private incomes differ as well, the solution had to include the distribution of the taxes among the two. In other words a choice of the best or most allocation of the two goods among the two individuals carry with it a distribution of the tax between the two individuals as decided upon by the distribution branch of the budget.

The solution to the efficiency problem, although solved with the aid of diagrams and mathematics, is but an economist's representation based on the tools at his disposal. In reality, the problem is a great deal more complicated for a number of reasons, the most significant being that society consists of many individuals whose preferences are not known to the budget authority. Moreover, since individuals differ with respect to their income and wealth, a choice on the utility frontier whereby the tax share allocation is explicitly introduced rests on the assumption of a given redistribution that is somehow determined by the distribution branch. Obviously other distributions can be made in the model, and different allocation can be obtained, but still the problem would remain. In short, in the absence of a mechanism for the revelation of individuals' preferences and an explicit distributional goal, the choice of a point on the utility frontier is as good as another.

It is to be remembered that the problem of allocation of the public good between the two individuals does not arise due to the nature of the social want. As defined earlier, the characteristics of a social want (public good) are such that the amount of the good is available to all; the exclusion principle does not exist. Thus, whatever is provided is available to both individuals. The only division applied to the private good.

The revelation problem along with the problem associated with the determination of the proper, or equitable distribution of incomes have plagued the economic discipline, especially at the applied level, as no universally accepted standard of equity has garnered the support of all individuals in society, at all times, and in all places.

Musgrave acknowledges these difficulties in his *Theory of Public Finance*. According to Musgrave, if indeed a need arises to redistribute private income and wealth, and for the fact that a "proper" distribution cannot be devised by relying on economic principles, the solution of this issue has to lie within the political process.

The Public Sector Budget

Returning to Musgrave's three branch model, it is clear that once their functions were identified, the next logical step is the incorporation of the budget of the three branches to come up with the overall budget of the public economy.

Musgrave in chapters 2 and 3 consolidated the goods provisions and the taxes that were raised to come up with the overall budget. In chapter 6, he offered an analysis of budget determination through voting. Although the overall budget formulation and execution is critical for the implementation of public sector's policy, the analysis he offered of this process took a back seat in the economic literature about the public economy, in contrast to his three branch model. Nonetheless, it needs to be pointed out that budget formulation is at the core of the budget-making process not only in the United States but throughout the world.

In any country, not only the United States, the debate during the budget process almost always centers on the overall level of budget expenditures and taxes, as these totals convey the use of private resources to meet the public economy's objectives. And, in light of our earlier discussion concerning the difficulties encountered in arriving at the true preferences of members of society, for both the level of provision of public goods and the distribution of the tax bill, budget formulation and implementation warrant more attention than what they received in the 1960s and 1970s following the publication of Musgrave's book. Indeed today, the biggest issue facing the public economy is budget allocation and the encroachment of the public economy on the functioning of the private economy. Musgrave's efforts in addressing the problems associated with budget formulation is perhaps one of the lasting contributions of his theory to our understanding of the functioning of the public economy. We turn next to the political modeling of the public economy.

Buchanan and Tullock: *The Calculus of Consent*

"With the Philosophers of the Enlightenment We share the faith that man can rationally organize his own society" (Buchanan and Tullock, 1965, p.306).

In the preface to their book, Buchanan and Tullock stated that their book is about the "Political organization of a society of freemen," and that their aim is to analyze the "calculus of the rational individual as he faces constitutional questions".

Early in the volume they made the point that economists spent an ordinate amount of time analyzing the individual decisions in the private market economy, and that social scientists did not address the process by which the individual arrives at decisions as a member of a social group.

Essentially, according to Buchanan and Tullock's thesis, what has been neglected is the process that "bridges" the gap between the individual choice calculus and group decisions. *The Calculus of Consent* addresses this neglect.

Buchanan and Tullock's *The Calculus of Consent* is a monumental study of collective actions. Their framework moves us logically and consistently from a sphere where the individual cares only about solving his own "maximization problem" by his actions in the private market economy, to a sphere where, as a member of a social group, he faces a maximization problem that is not totally under his control. Unlike the market where the costs and benefits are internal to the individual, in group-decision or collective action, benefits and costs are separated, that is who benefits may not be the one who bears the cost and vice versa.

The framework of analysis of the public economy employed in *The Calculus of Consent* differs significantly from that used by Musgrave and Samuelson. To begin with, Buchanan and Tullock questioned the prevailing conception of the state. They argued that, first of all one needs to pose the question: "What the state ought to be versus what the state is." Given that the state or the government is the instrument through which public sector activities take place, it is of the essence that whatever definition is offered, it should be understood.

As our concern in this chapter is with the provision of public goods and the distribution of tax shares imposed by the public sector to defray the cost of the provision, we shall limit ourselves to the task of presenting the alternative framework set forth in *The Calculus of Consent* in addressing these issues. This presentation by its limitations does not convey to the reader the full extent of the perspective that Buchanan and Tullock share about the public economy. Nonetheless, our presentation, limited as it might be, offers the readers sufficient information to grasp how the alternative model of the public economy stands against the traditional model.

Buchanan and Tullock: Modeling of the State

In the economist's standard model of the public economy, it is commonly assumed that the state or the government exists as a *separate* entity from individual members of the society. That its actions, expenditures, and taxation do not arise from market-type exchanges between the state and the individual. Buchanan and Tullock do not share this view—the state does not exist as a separate entity. Rather, it should be conceived as a "set of rules or institutions" through which individuals act collectively (1965, p.308). In other words, they dismiss the notion that the state is an entity separate from individuals. In their view, the decisions regarding collective goods provision and the cost sharing of their provision rest with the individual acting as a member of a social group.

To describe the process by which decisions for the provision of public goods takes place, they have put forth what they have labeled a "theory of political constitution". The theory is based on an analysis of "specific rules" for collective action under the standard economists' assumptions about human behavior. These assumptions are first, that in any decision, individuals are the relevant decision makers; second, that all individuals in the collectivity are capable of making choices; and third, that the "representative" (average) individual, as well as his fellows in the group, is motivated by self-interest.

Given these assumptions, it is clear that the principles used by Buchanan and Tullock to describe the public economy, the state are the same as those used by economists to describe the individual's behavior in the private market.

Recall that the basic assumption made by the economists is that the individual, motivated by self-interest, engages in exchanges for his own gains. In the private economy, a "utility-maximizing" individual recognizes only his benefits and costs from the exchange; the interests of all other individuals do not enter in his calculus of cost and benefit.

Buchanan and Tullock adopt this individualistic view in formulating their theory of collective choice. They advance the argument that just as in the case of economic relationships, in political relationships individuals in collective action join forces in order that they may achieve maximum gain. In other words, the forces that motivate individuals to make choices in the private economy are the same as those that motivate them when making choices in the public economy. In both instances they pursue "self-interest for maximum gain".

Given that their framework of analysis differs significantly from the standard public finance framework, those of Musgrave and Samuelson, it was natural for Buchanan and Tullock to begin by posing the most fundamental question of how the state ought to be conceived.

Conception of the State

Before answering the question they have posed, Buchanan and Tullock raised few objections about what constitutes, in their view, some common conceptions of the state. One of those is the "organic" conception of society, which postulates the emergence of a "mystical general will". Another conception of the state or the collectivity embodies the exploitation of a ruled by a ruling class. No matter which of these conceptions have been advanced, Buchanan and Tullock rejected any conception of state activity that divides the social group into a ruling class and an oppressed class.

Having rejected these common conceptions of the state, they offered instead "an individualist" conception of the collectivity. Accordingly, they replaced the concept of the state by the concept of "collective action" where collective action is the action of individuals when they choose to accomplish tasks collectively rather than individually (p.13). The state, or the government, in their view is nothing more than a "machine," an apparatus that permits collective action to take place. Thus, they advanced the following propositions:

- The state is a construct made by man. It is an artifact.
- The state, created by man, is subject to change; for better or worse.
- A constitutional change is judged an "improvement" if it can be shown to be in the interest of all parties.
- In the event the existing "constitution" required modification, then an improvement can be achieved (through what Buchanan and Tullock referred to as) conceptual unanimity.

Next, Buchanan and Tullock addressed the role of the individual in such a setting.

The Individual in the Social Choice Model

Economists usually speak of individuals' behavior in situations they face, whether in market transactions or in any other personal activities that they behave rationally. By rationality is meant that the individual, when faced with a choice, will choose the option that maximizes his gain. In terms of collective action—how to view the individual in this milieu? In other words, who is the decision maker? Is the individual the decision maker or is it the collectivity? The view espoused by Buchanan and Tullock is that only the "individual" chooses—that rationality is only meaningful for assessing the individual action. Within this individualistic framework, the assumption of individual rationality together with collective choice, the following principles may be derived:

- Collective action arises from individual actions.
- The individual will find it profitable to organize an activity collectively when he expects that the organization will increase his gain.
- Collective action may secure for the individual external benefits that may not be feasible through private action.
- The individual's utility from any collective activity is maximized when his share in the net cost of organizing the activity is minimized.
- In the absence of decision-making cost, the individual will support always the unanimous consent rule prior to the collective choice.
- In making a collective choice, only the unanimity rule will guarantee that external costs are eliminated.

If one were to accept the Buchanan-Tullock individualistic framework for the analysis of public sector activities, there need not be a concern about ethical issues arising from collective action, since individuals will only participate in collective choices if such choices are beneficial to them. A collective choice by definition yields gain to the individual participating in the collective decision. As Buchanan and Tullock emphasized, their views about the rational individual's ethics and morality differs from those developed throughout history.

Buchanan and Tullock expounded the notion of the "realm of social choice" by tying the benefits derived under collective choice to the cost of collective decision. In their chapter 5, they define benefits as the cost reduction from the level which would have been incurred had the activity been organized differently." The first element refers to those costs that the individual is expected to shoulder as a result of the actions of others (externalities cost); the second element of costs refers to the cost associated with the decision referred to as the "decision making costs".

To illustrate how these two types of costs arise, they gave an example of an activity undertaken by the individual as a private activity. It involves a choice of "red color underwear". Clearly this private choice of the individual does not impose an external cost on any member of his social group, although it may involve a private decision cost to the individual (to wear red or blue!). Buchanan and Tullock do not dwell on this private cost, as none is imposed on others. The decision-making costs are defined as the cost of participating in decisions when two or more individuals are required to reach an agreement (p.46).

Summing up the external costs and the decision costs of participating in group decision, they arrive at a sum referred to as the cost of social interdependence, or, simply interdependence costs. This value defines the individual participation in collective decisions—his goal is to reduce this interdependence costs when considering making institutional and constitutional changes.

Having defined the costs, the next logical step is to define the benefits. These benefits are referred to as "expected utility from social interdependence". The individual calculus, then, is to minimize this cost. Thus, for any activity, the individual engages in two types of calculations:

the first has to do with cost he would have incurred if the activity were left in the "realm of private choice"; the second is the expected minimum present value of total costs expected to be imposed by collective action (p.50). For a whole range of activities the individual is involved in the ranking of his choice. This ranking order is similar to the ranking the individual is engaged to in ordering market choices.

By comparing the various ranking of collective choice, the individual arrives at the "optimal" choice. That is, which activity is purely "individualistic," hence left to private choice, and which activity should be collectivized.

Of note is the fact that there exist some types of activities that do not obey the purely private action. For these types of activities (neighborhood watch, for example), voluntary arrangements may be the preferred solution. Buchanan and Tullock present cases where such an arrangement is effective whenever it minimizes the cost of decision. The individual calculus, therefore involves ordering. Once the ordering set is arrived at, the rational individual compares the expected costs of voluntary arrangements with expected costs of collective actions. In their views, the voluntary arrangement will always be more desirable except in cases where the "collective action is more efficient".

The implication of this calculus is that "the existence of external effects (externalities) of private behavior is "neither a necessary nor a sufficient condition for an activity to be placed in the realm of collective choice" (p.60). In their view, voluntary cooperation may remove all external effects. Nonetheless, they admit that in certain cases, the costs of voluntary action may exceed the costs of collective decision.

The Choice of Decision Rules

A collective choice by definition means that members of a group must participate in the decision. The framework for a group decision differs significantly from the market decision in that it requires that for any action to be taken that someone beside the individual must participate. If more than one individual has to agree on a decision, then there arises a "cost" for reaching such a decision. The decision cost clearly depends on the size of the group; the larger the group size whose agreement needs to be secured, the higher the cost of the decision. If the decision rule selected is "unanimity," then as unanimity is approached "dramatic increases in expected decision-making costs may be predicted" (p.68).

Having acknowledged that a "unanimous" decision entails a significant cost (and one might add that it would take only one member of the group to object, that individual refusal to agree would prevent the decision being reached), it was critical for Buchanan and Tullock to address the optimality of decision rules.

The choice of an optimal rule involves two key elements: the expected external costs (present values), which depend on the number of individuals needed to take a collective action (this type of cost falls as the number of individuals increases); the second, is the decision making cost (present value) that the individual incurs in participating in the decision (this cost rises as the number of individuals increases).

Given these two elements of costs, each of which is related to group size, the optimal decision rule is arrived at when the sum of these costs is at a minimum. Note that one of the two costs is falling; the other rising. A minimum point is reached when the reduction in cost exceeds the rise, and at this minimum value the group size gives the optimal rule.

The minimum cost analysis presented above gives an optimal rule that falls short of unanimity. Under such a decision rule, actions of others may impose costs at least on one individual. In other words, short of unanimous consent, the individual cannot be assured that the actions of others do not impose costs on him.

Note however that this is not to be the end of the individual decision-making calculus. As discussed above, participating in a collective decision suggests that the rational individual, in making a choice, compares the cost of private action with the cost of collective action. Participating in the collective decision suggests, *prima facia* that the cost of private action did exceed that of the collective action.

What collective activity should be provided? This question was taken up next in the *Calculus of Consent*. In the traditional analysis of public sector's activities, presented earlier in this chapter, we have identified the types of goods that would be provided by the public sector (the state): these are pure public goods and merit goods.

Buchanan and Tullock deal with this provision by examining those categories of governmental or collective activities that, in their views should be subject to "specific decision rules". Accordingly, they classified governmental activities into separate fields: those collective activities or "public" decisions that alter or restrict individuals property rights, where these rights were defined and accepted by the community. The decision rule in this case is closer to unanimity to protect the rights of the citizen that were hitherto secured.

The second category includes all or most of the activities characteristically undertaken by governments: examples are education, fire protection, police protection, and the like, all of which fall in the traditional public goods category. In their analysis, as was the case in traditional public finance; the government is called upon to provide those goods, commonly referred to as pure public goods. Buchanan and Tullock's exposition in *The Calculus of Consent* seems to be in agreement with the traditional public finance contention that the cost of provision of these types of goods by far exceeds the ability of one individual or a group of individuals to pay for their provision.

If the provision of these pure public goods is to be left to the state, or the public sector, the individual, as far as he can recognize the costs and impact of such decision, will try to choose a decision rule that is less than "unanimity".

The implication of the Buchanan-Tullock analysis may be summarized as follows (pp.81-82):

- It is rational to have a constitution. It is rational for the individual to choose more than one decision rule.
- There will be no constitution, if there is only a single rule.
- The rule of unanimity possesses certain special attributes; only through this rule the individual can insure that no external damage will be inflicted upon him through the action of others.
- Majority rule ($N/2+1$), or 51 per cent of the voting population is not unique. It is one amongst many possible rules.
- The individual's support of a shift of an activity from the public sector to the private sector (and vice versa), will depend on the decision-making rule that is to prevail in the collective action.

The Range and Extent of Collective Action

The public economy, as noted earlier in the Musgrave-Samuelson models is called upon to meet through its provisions social wants. The type of wants to be provided and the extent of the provision in Musgrave's treatise are determined by the allocation branch of the budget. In the Buchanan and Tullock's *Calculus*, a distinction is made between the "range" of activities and the "extent" to which these activities may be "pushed". In other words, not only does the composition of social wants matter, but also how far the satisfaction of these wants should be pursued. According to Buchanan and Tullock, these are separate issues that are to be considered in arriving at a collective decision (p.205).

When the question arises as to the allocation of society's resources between the public or collective sector and the private sector of the economy, a distinction has to be made between the ranges of activities that would be collectivized and the extent to which they ought to be. This distinction, according to Buchanan and Tullock, is often overlooked.

According to Buchanan-Tullock, if the decision rule falls short of unanimity, any public goods provision will tend to either be "unduly restricted" or "unduly expanded" compared to a benchmark.

Their significant conclusions may be stated as follows:

- The decision as to whether or not a specific activity that is in the nature of public good should or should not be organized in the public economy will depend on the decision-making rule chosen (p.207).
- The individual in his capacity as a constitutional maker chooses first the fundamental organization of the activity—private versus public—and then chooses the decision-making rule (p.210).
- That the ideal organization of activities of the public economy may embody many and varying rules for making collective decisions and may involve considerable decision costs.
- Social organization in which man (some men or all men) is allowed the exercise of free choice will not prevent the exploitation of man-by-man or group by another group (p.304).
- Replacing a market organization by political organization does not eliminate an opportunity for some individuals to impose external costs on others.

On an optimistic note, Buchanan and Tullock suggested that even though organizational norms are based on the view that group behavior gives rise to external costs imposed on one group of individuals, others may be channeled in such a direction that their behavior may be beneficial to the interests of all members of the collectivity (p.304).

By way of conclusion, they raise the question: Can the pursuit of individual self-interest be turned into the greater good in politics as well as in economics? Buchanan and Tullock believed it to be so.

Summary

The basic ingredients of the public economy may be summarized as consisting of three elements: a definition of the major actor—the state; the functions of the state; and the implications of the state's actions for the private economy.

The history of economic thought offered contrasting views of the state; its functions but fell short of outlining a framework within which these functions could be carried out.

From the classical economists of the eighteenth and nineteenth centuries to modern day economists, the question that received most of the attention is the role of the state. The definition of what the state is, or how it should be conceived did not matter for defining the functions ascribed to the state. All that was needed is the knowledge that the state is a Sovereign that possesses power over individuals. In this capacity it exercised a very "visible hand" over the economic life of individuals. It has extended beyond the extraction of private resources to fund its activities to imposing rules that govern individuals' behavior in the public economy.

Since the state did not possess resources of its own that could be used to fund its activities, however conceived, the classical economists devoted an inordinate amount of time and effort to the analysis of taxation—the major source of revenues to the Sovereign. Their analysis extended beyond simply identifying bases on which taxes were to be levied to providing a comprehensive evaluation of the effects of the various forms of taxations on the tax bases. Their perceptions in setting out principles that should stand the test of time and place are remarkable to say the least. They have established the foundations for tax incidence; a subject that is of major concern to micro economists as they pursue the analysis of price determination and the allocation of resources.

The major omission fell on the expenditure side of the public economy. This omission, for the most part, reflected the classical economists' views, fashioned along Adam Smith's notion of the invisible hand. The functions they assigned to the state or the sovereign were quite limited, which was also consistent with the view that the sovereign's decisions should not replace individuals' decisions. It supported the notion that wealth creation is the product of individuals' initiatives and that the state should not alter those incentives.

The vision of an active public economy sprang from the political economist's concerns for fairness and equitable access for the most disadvantaged groups to society's resources. Two major developments in the science of economics, welfare economics, and macroeconomics, set the stage for the development of a new theory of the public economy. It was no longer feasible to discuss taxation without resorting to some norms such as the equity of the distribution of the tax burden, along with the acknowledgment that tax revenues have to be used for the public good.

As the presentation of the literature reviewed in this chapter, although modest tried to convey, a comprehensive view of the public economy did not take hold in the study of economics until the twentieth century through the efforts of Musgrave and Samuelson. Musgrave integrated the separate activities of the public sector by emphasizing the three functions of the public economy—reallocation of resources, redistribution of private income and wealth, and stabilization of the aggregate economy.

In the twentieth century, the public sector was no longer viewed as an add-on to the private economy, but rather as a third element that is as important to the functioning of the economy as the other two—the individual consumer and the business firm—the producer.

Unlike the analysis of the private market economy, an analysis of the state, from the conception of what it is to the activities it performs, is fraught with difficulties as it lacks the consensus of political economists, politicians, and the public at large about not only its role in the economy but also the extent to which its activities ought to be extended. Another, perhaps more fundamental concern in democratic societies is the process by which the state's activities are determined in the first place and the type of rules that should be followed to insure that the individual, rather than an "organic" creation, is the decision maker. Constitutional rules, it is argued, not only guarantees that the individual and not an organic concept of the state is the decision maker, but that well-conceived rules would protect the exploitation of the majority by a minority.

The public choice school, a relatively new, twentieth-century school of political economy enriched the economist's knowledge of the process of decision making when the collectivity replaces the individual as the decision maker. The public choice school, when put in the frame of reference of those political economists dating back to the eighteenth century, has without a doubt changed the landscape for the study of the public economy.

The thesis advanced in *The Calculus of Consent*, by its focus on the individual as the decision maker in the public economy, has moved us not back to the world of Adam Smith but forward to a world where one need not look beyond the motivations of individuals to formulate or arrive at policies that touch the lives of individuals, whether those are tax or expenditure policies.

Buchanan and Tullock's teachings go well beyond our modest objective in this chapter, as we seek to link their teachings to what was put forth about the public economy centuries ago. The treatise advanced there goes beyond our modest and brief presentation in this chapter, as it put forth constitutional rules for collective action. *The Calculus of Consent*, which has been cited by the Nobel Committee as a significant contribution to the study of political economy in general and public choice in particular, will undoubtedly transform the study of the public economy in the twenty-first century and beyond.

Students of the public economy, we believe, will shift their focus from the analysis of issues such as tax principles and the character of public goods and their provision, to uncover the modes of behavior of those who govern and those who are governed. This line of inquiry will enhance our understanding of the role of the individual as he interacts with the sovereign in matters that are important to his own welfare and the welfare of those who share with him the outcome of collective action.

The twenty-first century offers political economists the opportunity to widen their knowledge about the "elusive role" of the state. *The Calculus of Consent* has paved the way toward such knowledge.

7   WHAT ECONOMISTS DO

"Economists study the actions of individuals but study them in relation to social rather than individual life—they watch carefully the conduct of a whole class of people, sometimes the whole of a nation, in all this they deal with man, as he is not with an abstract or Economic man."

—Alfred Marshall *Principles of Economics*
(1890 [1948], pp.25-26).

It is by now clear to the readers that the name of Adam Smith will adorn every essay on the subject of economics. To answer the question of what economists do, we need, first of all, to identify the first person the title of "economist" has been bestowed upon. Paul Samuelson, a Nobel laureate in economics (1970), named Adam Smith the first economist (*The Collected Scientific Papers of Paul Samuelson*, Stiglitz ed., Vol 2, 1966, p.1409). No one in the economics profession, then or now, is likely to disagree with Samuelson's tribute to Adam Smith.

From our journey through the history of economic thought, the tribute to Adam Smith rests not on his identity, a Scottish fellow, born in the town of Kirkcaldy, county of Fife, Scotland in the year 1723, or because Dr. Smith was a "professor" at the University of Glasgow lecturing on problems of "Moral Philosophy," a subject that covered "Natural Theology, Ethics, Jurisprudence and Political Economy"; rather because of his "insights" about the human actions and the environment that surrounds them.

Prior to the publication of *An Inquiry into The Wealth of Nations,* Smith, the "social Philosopher," published a book (perhaps not as well known to students of economics as the Inquiry) in 1759 entitled *The Theory of Moral Sentiment.* The book established Smith at the forefront of English philosophers. Seventeen years later in 1776, Smith's *Wealth of Nations* was published. The book, called a masterpiece, earned Smith the designation of the first economist and ranked Smith not only among his contemporaries but also through the centuries, as the "economist", the initiator of the science of economics.

One might ask then what the first economist did during the year 1776. Aside from being a lecturer, a teacher, and a writer, Adam Smith was the economist who shaped the individual's views about who he is as he interacts with his fellow human beings and for himself to guard against a long and a, far-reaching, visible hand of the sovereign.

His two volumes, *An Inquiry into the Wealth of Nations* and *The Moral Sentiments,* stand today as living monuments to the intellect of the economist. Smith's intellectual genius paved the way for others—the economists to travel not as sightseers, but as builders and promoters of values that, above all, address the basic problem of man's survival as a member of a social group (see chapter 2, this volume). A quotation from Heilbroner (1953) illustrates this idea: "Smith has constructed for society a giant endless chain—from its starting point accumulation of wealth will take place, and this accumulation will result in increased facilities for production and in a greater division of labour". With division of labor, wealth is augmented.

What was foreseen by Smith was not a utopia but a program of action. Smith words to the "wise": the market must be left free, all impediments to the market must go; whatever interferes with the market does so at the expense of wealth creation.

Smith, the economist, could not have come up with the notion of self-interest and economic freedom without a deep understanding of human nature, human motivations, pain, sadness, and joy. His treatise on moral sentiment gave him insight into human motivation—insight without which he, the economist, would not have been able to prescribe to man how to solve his survival problem as a member of his social group.

To be an economist demands a great deal of knowledge, not just about the tools of trade, but knowledge of the subject for whom the science came to be developed. Man is a complex being; he is not an "island to himself," but interacts with his social group in so many different settings and has to solve his survival problem within the constraints imposed by a collectivity, whose values may not coincide with his own.

Economics as a Profession

George Stigler, in his collected papers published in 1965 under the title, "Essays in The History of Economics," took on the task of enumerating attributes that define the economist. Economics is a profession; hence the economist is a professional man. In the words of Stigler: "A professional man is one who supports himself by the activity in question" (p.32). In the case of the economist, he supports himself through the practice of economics. But income is not the only reason the economist pursues his profession. Stigler gives the example of David Ricardo, who was diligent and single-minded in his pursuit of economics, although he was also quite successful as a stockbroker. John Stuart Mill, another notable economist, on the other hand, could not support himself and his wife by being an economist. He was obliged to take on a job as a journalist and was financially aided by a fellow economist. Robert Malthus, another famous economist, who was un-prosperous and lived modestly driving his income from college teaching.

Stigler identifies two attributes that define the professional economist: specialization and persistence. The professional economist is not a "general practitioner"; he must concentrate his efforts in a specific area of study where he acquires expertise—the required techniques needed for his specialization. Persistence is a part of the course. The professional economist must pursue with diligence the knowledge and applications that pertains to his specialization.

Given that the majority of professional economists derive their income from the practice of their profession, the level of income depends on their success in accumulating and disseminating the knowledge they acquire through specialization and persistence. The economist does not cure an ill person; neither does he flies an airplane (although some of us do) for gain. The fact that the income received is the return on the economist's effort, this effort has to be identified and measured. In other words the economist's "output" has to be quantified. As will be discussed later on in the chapter, economists play many roles, such as university teacher, political economist, adviser to politicians, and advisor to businesses, and so on. Each one of these engagements has its own measure of the contribution of the economist and consequently his compensation.

The most widely used measure of the output of the economist is his scholarly activities. For a university professor at all levels, from assistant professor to a full professor, there are two measurements that are applied: publications and educated students. Until the mid-1970s, the only indicator used for measuring the economist's output was scholarly publications. The educational attainment of students is not the sole product of one teacher; it is the product of the teaching of so many, and therefore it is not exclusively the value added of the economist. As to publication, the author is the sole contributor. With advances in samples techniques, design of questionnaires, and analyses of responses, almost all colleges and universities have become reliant on students' responses to evaluate teachers' output and thus for setting their rates of return.

Although, the value added of the economist (or any other teacher for that matter), is the raison d'être for attending a class in economics, in most cases the economist's value added is not scored in correspondence with this value added. Publication in scholarly journals earns the highest score in appraising the contribution of the economist and hence his remunerations.

To reinforce the practice of placing scholarly publication at the top of the achievement the Nobel Prize Committee selects Nobel laureates solely on the basis of their scientific contributions to the discipline through the medium of scholarly publications. No one has ever heard of a Nobel laureate in economics being awarded the prize on the strength of his teaching or his value-added to the educational attainments of his students.

Scholarly publications should indeed be valued and ranked at the top of whatever scale one might use to measure the value added of the economist. Through his publications, the economist creates "scientific knowledge". As Stigler put it, "The pre-eminence of publication has various bases. It is deemed a greater achievement to produce knowledge than to communicate it" (1965, p.33).

Economists on Economists

In preparing for our journey through the history of economic thought, we have chosen for ourselves the road on which we travel. The road led us to those who in our views have established economics as a "science," and whose contributions stand today as firm and as vigorous as they did three centuries ago. Smith, Malthus, Ricardo, Mill, Walras, and Marshall were among the early founders of the discipline of economics. What we put forth in this volume are those principles of economics—the building blocks upon which contributors of succeeding generations were to build upon. The twentieth-century economists built their own theories, not from the ground floor, but from where their predecessors labored, picking and choosing, rehabilitating some of the classical theories (See Keynes on the classical economists, chapter 5 in this volume), discarding others, and, for the most part, reinventing and/or reinforcing the basic tenets of the discipline.

Having established in the previous chapters what our forefathers have created, it is time to look at them, not as the great scholars that they were, but rather as men whose trade was economics and as members of a group we refer to as the "Economists".

Paul Samuelson, in his presidential address, "Economists and the History of Ideas," delivered at the Seventy Fourth Annual meeting of the American Economic Association (December 27, 1961), offered his audience a sharp and witty assessment of the founding fathers of the science of economics. Through a "Looking Glass", he presented two contrasting views about the classical economists. These views were expressed in two volumes: *The History of Economic Analysis* by Joseph Schumpeter; the other Guide and Rist: *A History of Economic Doctrines*. In addition to this review, Samuelson offered his own assessment of the key figures in the classical tradition—Smith, Malthus, and Ricardo—as well as non-classical economists especially Marshall and Keynes.

Conflicting judgments about the ranking of a scholar or the ingenuity of an idea are to be expected in any discipline. Most often, they are welcomed in that differing judgments induce many in a discipline to reassess what they have learned or thought they have learned, thereby extending the knowledge beyond the original ideas, and maybe even giving birth to new ones.

The judgments of Schumpeter and, Guide and Rist, as relayed by Samuelson to his audience, are of great value in that they highlighted the developments of the doctrines of economics and who's who among Heilbroner's *The Worldly Philosophers*. On these judgments rests not only the professional survivability of the individual being judged, but also the survival of the principles he has advocated. Since Smith, in the words of Samuelson, was the first economist, it is of interest to know how he fared in the judgment of the twentieth century economists, notably Schumpeter, Guide and Rist, Heilbroner, and Samuelson.

Guide and Rist delivered a judgment about few classical economists that stood apart from that given by Schumpeter. Guide and Rist did not, in their ranking of these economists, place a high value on the contributions made by Malthus or Walras compared to the ranking they ascribed to lesser known economists of their century. Schumpeter, too, offered a most unexpected ranking in his identification of the "greatest economists of the world". Schumpeter singled out four economists as the greatest; of these four, three were Frenchmen and the fourth was an Englishman.

As Samuelson relayed to his fellow economists attending his presidential address the ranking of Schumpeter, the expectation was that Adam Smith would be among his four greatest economists in the world. Not so; Alfred Marshall took the prize. The three Frenchmen were: Walras, Cournot, and Quesnay.

Samuelson gave his audience his own assessment of some economists in the classical tradition, as well. In his looking glass, Smith stood on a pinnacle. Samuelson believed Smith to be underrated as an economic theorist, and also that his impact could not be understated as a political economist (*Collected Scientific Papers*, 1966, p.1505).

Samuelson went on to rate several other economists. Of the classical economists we have written about their contributions throughout this volume, Samuelson did not spare any from his sharp wit, praise, or critique. He described Ricardo as a "whipping boy" for continental philosophers and historians, although he also praised him for his remarkable theory of comparative advantage, describing it as "his greatest tour de force". Still, Samuelson's overall assessment of Ricardo was not salutary referring to him as "the most overrated economist" of the time.

Samuelson describes Mill as a "thinker and reflector". He laments the fact that Mill's contributions were ignored, and his presence in the economic sphere as a "transitional figure". The timing of Mill's publication of his *Principles of Political Economy* (1848) could not have been worse, in that at the same time of the publication of his volume and his exposition of his social philosophy, there appeared on the scene another treatise: Karl Marx's *Das Kapital*. In *Das Kapital*, Marx preached a "social Philosophy" that became known as socialist economics. Marx launched a vicious attack on Mill's social views, and although Marx's views were contradicted by economic events, Mill did not overcome the critique, and his contributions were all but forgotten.

Another blow to Mill's theories came from a different quarter. The appearance of a very significant contribution by the "Marginalist school of thought" of Jevons, Walras, and Menger, which took the discipline of economics further in developing scientific analysis of utility, an analysis that is fundamental to the consumption and demand theories, as well as welfare economics.

Samuelson's harshest judgment was reserved for Alfred Marshall. Marshall was a neoclassical economist. His volume, *Principles of Economics* was published in 1890. Marshall's text is read by more students of economics than Smith's *Wealth of Nations*. That did not mean, at least to Samuelson, that Marshall's work should be viewed as a worthy contribution in the manner in which one considers the *Wealth of Nations*. Samuelson queries his listeners: "What has been Marshall's role in the history of economics? What was Marshall's influence over his long life on the educated man of affairs?" To these questions he offered an answer: "Marshall thought he was writing for the businessman, but anyone who looks at the *Principles* would realize that no businessman, in good Queen Victoria's time or since would be likely to find it attractive" (*Collected Scientific Papers*, 1966, p.1514).

In an essay published in 1946 and reproduced in his *Collected Scientific Papers*, Samuelson took on the task of evaluating the man and his theory, John Maynard Keynes, a twentieth century economist. Samuelson presented an overview of the life, work, academic and non-academic, of Keynes as well as positions that he held in academia, and in the service for his government. He also pointed out the accolades heaped on him, and whatever else that describe the essence of the man, "the economist".

Being about as famous to twentieth century students of economics as Adam Smith is, there is not much of a chance that a student of economics is likely to forget about who Keynes was. To some, he was the savior of the economic order; to others he was the preacher of doom. Samuelson's review of some facet of the life and works of Keynes needed to be put before students of economics, especially those who had but a few glimpses of Keynes's other contributions (such as *The Indian Currency and Finance* and *The Economic Consequences of Peace*). In addition to his review of the life and work of Keynes, Samuelson offered us a judgment about an economist's work by a fellow economist of the first caliber; a Nobel Prize winner as the time was to testify.

Reading Samuelson's assessment of Keynes, one is taken aback by Samuelson's description of *The General Theory*. He wrote: "It is badly written book, poorly organized, any layman who, being led by the author's previous reputation, bought the book was cheated of his five shilling." But one should not stop there. Further reading of Samuelson assessment of Keynes's *General Theory* corrects this unflattering impression. Samuelson added: "In it, the Keynesian system stands out indistinctly, flashes of insights and intuition interpose tedious algebra—when finally mastered, its analysis is found to be obvious and at the same time new—in short, it is a *work of genius*" (1966, p.1521).

Heilbroner in his volume: *The Worldly Philosophers* (1953) provides us with an intimate look at the life and contributions of the following economists *cum* philosophers of the past four centuries: Smith, Malthus, Ricardo, Marx, Veblen, and Keynes. Below we relayed what he saw, in his "looking glass" for the three classical economists; Smith, Malthus, and Ricardo. Heilbroner's assessment of the contributions of these three differed significantly from those offered by Guide and Rist, Schumpeter, and Samuelson.

For Heilbroner, Smith's *Inquiry* was, unquestionably a masterpiece. Even though he admits that many of Smith's ideas were not new—"he did not discover the market," others had. Smith nonetheless, according to Heilbroner, was "the first to understand the full philosophy of action, which such a conception demanded; the first to formulate the entire scheme, in a wide and systematic fashion . . . and he was the first to build an edifice of social order on the understanding he achieved".

Heilbroner's views on Malthus and Ricardo were not always flattering; sometimes his judgment was even downright unpleasant. Although he viewed Malthus's theory of rent, which predated Ricardo's theory of rent which was put forth in 1820, as a remarkable contribution, describing Malthus as a "foremost economist," he nonetheless labeled him, and Ricardo, as preachers of doom. He attributed to them the vision of a "gloomy world"—a view that elicited an everlasting designation of economics as the "dismal science".

Comparing Ricardo's and Malthus's world with the world of Smith, Heilbroner contrasted the vision of society as portrayed by Smith to the vision seen by Ricardo and Malthus. The society projected by Smith was one of a great family, whereas Ricardo saw it as a bitter contest for supremacy; Malthus's vision of society was even worse. He saw society "caught in hopelessness in which the human reproductive urge would inevitably push humanity to the sheer brink of the precipice of existence" (Heilbroner, 1953, p.70).

George Stigler lent a hand in rendering judgments of economists on economists. In his *Essays* (1965), Stigler first of all, linked scientific progress to the "originality" of scientific ideas. Such originality would be measured against the "knowledge of man's contemporaries". Thus, if an economist was instrumental in opening the eyes of his fellow contemporary economists to new ideas or new perspective on old ones, then he is an "original" economist. Being original earned the economist the title of a "great" economist. By this criterion, Stigler labeled Smith, Ricardo, Walras, Marshall, and Keynes as great economists; they have, in Stigler view, "changed the beliefs and interests of economists" (Stigler, 1965, p.4).

Applying the originality criterion to our select group of economists, Stigler singled out John Stuart Mill as being undeservedly mislabeled as a mediocre economist, despite the fact that Mill was one of the "most original economists in the history of the science" (p.7). Robert Malthus, according to Stigler, was perhaps uncharitably treated by his fellow economists. His theory on population, according to Stigler had received a "most emphatic refutation any prominent economic theory has ever received". Stigler, nonetheless, insisted that Malthus deserved to be acknowledged for giving population its rightful place in economic theory.

David Ricardo seemed to elicit contradictory assessments of his contributions to scientific knowledge from the twentieth-century economists. Like Samuelson, Stigler first credits Ricardo for his insights on the law of diminishing returns (although Malthus was the first to put it forth), but does not credit him for enhancing the knowledge of the workings of the economic system. For Stigler, "Ricardo did not enlarge [this] body of knowledge". Nevertheless, Ricardo was praised by Stigler for his "naked logic; that his pseudo-logic helped to establish a professional frame of mind," which helped to "initiate order and precision in fact gathering". Stigler refers to Ricardo's logic as the basic "Ricardo's effect" (1965, p.197).

Stigler, like Schumpeter and Samuelson, praised Walras for his scientific contribution to the science of economics. As one of the founders of utility theory, along with Menger and Jevons, Walras was credited for laying out the foundations for the modern analyses of consumer choice and welfare theory. He was also credited for the development of a general equilibrium system of equations, hence introducing the mathematical method of analyses in the study of economics.

Keynes taught, wrote essays and treatises, assumed the editorship of the *Economic Journal*—Britain's most influential economic publication, offered advice to politicians at home and abroad, was praised by his teacher Alfred Marshall, in addition to other honors. He was "elevated to the peerage"; becoming Lord Keynes.

Seymour E. Harris's volume, *The New Economics*, first published in 1947, was devoted to the great economist Keynes. The volume contains thirty-four chapters covering Keynes's contributions to the science of economics. Contributors to the volume at that time were (still are) the most prestigious economists. Praise, as well as critique, was levied in the volume, not only with regards to his general theory, but also for his other contributions, especially his *Treatise on Money*. (A bibliography of Keynes's writing is contained in the Harris volume).

Harris's edited volume is remarkable in its coverage of some 700 pages devoted to Keynes. It would take a student of economics not one month, but more likely a year to absorb all that was written about the economic thoughts and economic policies put forth by Keynes in his many contributions. With the caveat that whatever we convey in this short space about the scholars assessments of Keynes's contributions, it is most likely to be inadequate.

The obituary of Keynes reported in *The Times* (London, April 22, 1946), described Lord Keynes as "A Great Economist . . . a man of genius, who as a political economist had a worldwide influence on the thinking both of the specialists and the general public."

To be an economist is a choice inspired by what economists do. Clearly, what an economist does is to follow a path that challenges his intellect and, in doing so, enlightens himself as well as those who follow his path. Many classical economists followed the path of their fathers (John Stuart Mill and Leon Walras). What they achieved was clearly dependent on the time during which they were born, the problems their societies faced, as well as a bit of luck and fortitude.

Whereas Keynes the economist taught economics to undergraduates at Kings' college and helped in the development of the economic faculty at Cambridge, wrote a treatise on political economy and economics, he was not always an academic. He joined the British Civil Service and held political positions in the British government. His fame, political appointments, and influence were clearly based on his contributions as an economist. As Alfred Marshall eloquently put it: the economist studies the actions of individuals in relation to societal life; he studies the whole of a nation. Keynes did just that. In his study of individuals and the nation, he developed theories and advocated policies that gained him recognition and accolades.

An economist aspires to do that, not always for praise or accolades, although he may seek them, but rather to be an agent for change; a change toward the enhancement of the life of the individual, his group, and his nation. Lord Keynes was one great economist among many. Having discussed the man, a few quotations from Harris's volume on Keynes are in order.

Alvin Hansen, one of the great economists who wrote about Keynes's contributions in the Harris volume, stated: "While it is not possible now to assess the ultimate place of Keynes in the history of economic thought, it is safe to say that no book in economics has ever made such a stir within the first ten years of its publication as *The General Theory*" (Harris, 1952, p.134). Another assessment was given by R. F. Harrods: "Keynes . . . was practical and a man of the world. He was a tremendous fighter, prepared to take on great odds, but he was not inclined to be a crusader for a merely utopian aim" (p.70). Another contributor, Paul Sweezy wrote: "If Keynes were to receive credit for nothing else . . . his title to fame would be secure" for he had opened up a new vista and a new pathway to a whole generation of economists (pp.105-106).

> Harris had nothing but praise of Keynes' *General Theory*: "Since 1935, literally thousands of economists all over the world have read the general theory and large numbers have examined it with painstaking care, and, in fact, subjected almost every paragraph to microscopic study. *The General Theory* has given birth to hundreds, if not thousands of articles—in fact there are, few books in general economics written since the 1936 that have not been influenced consciously or subconsciously by Keynes" (p.46).

It is perhaps ironic that Keynes was born in the same year that Karl Marx died. The irony is that Marx predicted the collapse of capitalism, whereas the economist that followed, Lord Keynes, was on the scene to rescue it. Beyond the first, the second, or the third economist, there are economists of many persuasions, prestige and "métier".

What Kind of Economists?

Economists are a diverse group. What economists do reflects not only the richness of the discipline but also depends on the environment wherein they practice their profession. Given that economists differ among themselves in training, interests and expertise, it would be foolish to state in one or few sentences what economists do as this would imply that "one size" fits all.

The fact that economists come in different sizes (not to be taken literally) the answer to the question posed, as to "what economists do", depends on which size one refers to.

The Political Economist

The most famous and perhaps the most sought-after job in any nation is that of the political economist. The job ranges from a much-coveted one as that of a president, a prime minister (for example in Greece and Italy), to that of a political appointment to a cabinet position such as the US Secretary of the Treasury, the Chairman of the President's Council of Economic Advisers; the Chairman of the Federal Reserve System, or a member of a political elite and/or the ruling class. Other lucrative positions include such appointment as the Head of the European Central Bank in the European Union, or the head of those prestigious organizations such as the International Monetary Fund or the World Bank.

Of course other coveted political jobs go to political economists, either as political appointees, or as advisers to presidents, prime ministers, cabinet secretaries, as well as to international agencies. In all such glamorous, well compensated and powerful positions, the political economist puts his discipline on the line, the stakes are quite high and so is the prestige of the economic profession in general, and the political economist in particular.

Success and failure are part of the course, as Mark S. Massel put it: "The economist functions within a nebulous operational framework. Though, he frequently must make predictions, there can be no clear determinations of his success or failure" (Massel, 1959, p.142).

Being a political economist does not always mean serving as an "upper echelon" political adviser. Most often, the label refers to an economist whose opinions are sought-after by the political establishment. Nobel laureates in economics are constantly asked for their opinions on many issues, from the current state of the economy and forecasts about its future path, to the state of the world economies and the future outlook for specific nations or the global economy.

Television interviews with Nobel laureates and political economists holding political positions, often adorn pages of prestigious papers and television stations in the United States as well as outside the United States. Indeed, the quotations about the future path of the national or global economy elicited from economists are limited only by the scarcity of Nobel laureates, and/or by political events that are not shaped by economic events. A testimony about the significance of economics and especially what political economists do fills the pages of *The Economist* a British magazine first published in September 1843 that is devoted mostly to the subject of economics, the research findings of economists, the views and opinions of economists in academia, as well as in political positions and in particular the effects of the science of economics on the lives of people in the global economy.

The title of political economist however is not a twentieth-century label. In fact, one would say that Adam Smith was a political economist having held a government appointment. Following the publication of his Inquiry in 1776, he was appointed in 1778 as "Commissioner of Customs for Edinburgh," not an elite political position to be sure, but a political position nonetheless.

Keynes of course may be considered a political economist, with or without a specific designation. In addition to holding positions in the British government, his influence on the world of economics and politics is well documented and written about.

But there are other economists whose contributions to the political scene cannot be overlooked. During the Second World War, many academic economists joined the US government as political economists to analyze the cost of the war and its effects on the level of output and employment. Economists in other countries were called upon as well to do the same.

In the twenty-first century and beyond, the political economist will always be there, dispensing advice and offering solutions to his nation's economic problems and often the economic problems of other nations. Whether right or wrong, they will always be there.

Of the economists of the eighteenth and the nineteenth centuries we have discussed in this volume, neither Malthus, Ricardo, Mill,

Walras, nor Marshall held political appointments. They, along with the economists of the twentieth-century we have journeyed with in this volume—Samuelson, Musgrave, Buchanan and Tullock, belonged to a class of economists usually labeled scholars, teachers, writers, and businessmen.

Of note, is the fact that most political economists who occupy positions of note, have at one time or another, been in academia. The political economist does not spring from thin air; reputations are made (or lost) in the confines of the classroom, in written words, and in published articles and books.

What differentiates a political economist from the non-political economist is that they hold different values and commitments to their profession. An academic economist makes commitments to his profession, his college, and his students, as well as to himself. The political economist makes commitment to his government in his capacity as a political economist. He puts his knowledge at the disposal of his employer in the hope that his advice will be taken and that the policies he recommends, when implemented, would benefit not only his government and his nation but also the image of the economist, himself and his discipline.

The Academic Economist

The academician is an economist who fulfills a role similar to that fulfilled by others in the knowledge profession. He is an educator, a teacher, and in academia he is also a researcher with a publication record. His contribution to the education attainment of his students and to his science is valued in tangible ways; promotion to the highest rank in academia, the full professor rank, and a "pecuniary" return, determined by the scale of the various ranks in similarly situated institutions of higher learning, but most of all by the budgetary needs of the institution in relation to its resources.

For institutions of higher education, and especially those offering graduate education, outside sources of funds are critical for the quality of their offering, the faculty they attract and the reputation they acquire. Economists, at least most of them who are in academia by choice (Stigler refers to that as aversion to take jobs in business), have developed an economic concept to assure themselves that the choice they made by being in academia was the right one, even if opportunities outside academia were alluring. That concept is referred to as "none pecuniary return". In other words, what the academician receives in compensation cannot be measured solely by dollars and cents, but by the rewards that the teacher reaps in opening students' minds in developing their potential, and in enhancing the world around them.

Stigler (1965) put before us a catalog of English economists who in his view have had significant influence upon the economists of their times, covering the period 1766-1915. He classified these economists according to their occupation. His list encompasses fifty-six economists; foremost among them are Adam Smith (1766-1834); John Stuart Mill (1806-1873); David Ricardo (1772-1823); and Alfred Marshall (1842-1924). Of interest is the income source derived by Stigler's distinguished group of economists. Out of the fifty-four economists on the list, he enumerated, eleven of which were professors of economics, another thirty were economists that derived their income from teaching or writing on the subject of economics with records of publication (Stigler, 1965, pp.34-35).

Not all great economists of the period derived their income solely from work in academia or that the income received by some was adequate. As mentioned earlier, John Stuart Mill for one had to relinquish teaching to work as a journalist in order to support his family (his remuneration as a teacher was poor). On the other hand, Ricardo, a successful stockbroker and a landowner, did not derive his income from being an economist, although he was a prolific writer in the science of economics.

Walras and Marshal were two economists who belonged to the ranks of academic economists. Unlike Marshall, who was as big as life in his college at Cambridge, Walras had quite a time securing a position teaching economics or political economy in the country of his birth.

Born in 1834, in Evreux, in the Department of Eure, France, Leon Walras did not have a bit of luck during his students' adult years. Even though Walras's father was a distinguished economist, the subject of economics was not to his son's liking, ability, or interest. Leon Walras's success as an economist however, was gained by his sheer persistence and his intellect. He studied political economy on his own; he wrote papers on several economic issues, especially on taxation, yet he failed to secure a placement in academia in France. As luck would have it at this later stage of his career, he was invited to deliver a lecture at the Faculty of Law of the Academy of Lausanne. There, he delivered his taxation paper, which was so well received that few years later he was offered a chair in Economics at the Academy. He held that position until his retirement in 1892.

In his translation of Leon Walras's *Elements d'Economie Politique Pure*, William Jaffee, an American economist, gave Walras the credit for inspiring many great economists, including Pareto, Wicksell, Fisher, and Schumpeter; all of whom were viewed as the great economists of the twentieth-century.

Although recognized by his peers, Walras did not gain his rightful place among them. Few students of economics in American universities would know of him or had the privilege of reading his *Elements*. One reason perhaps is that, not until the 1950s, was an English translation made of his *Elements*. His contributions, however, did not go unnoticed. In 1892, the American Economic Association elected him as an honorary member in recognition of his "eminent" services to the science of political Economy. Walras kept on writing about matters of economics until his death in 1910.

The twentieth century economists whose contributions we have highlighted in this volume, besides John Maynard Keynes were Richard Musgrave, Paul Samuelson, James Buchannan, and Gordon Tullock. These economists represent the group of the "most distinguished" economists of the twentieth century.

It is beyond the confines of this volume to highlight the contributions of such distinguished academic economists to the science of economics. It suffices to say, that no student of economics, either at the undergraduate or the graduate level, did not have the privilege of knowing these illustrious scholars, through their work, lectures, and publications. Their occupations as economists in academia, their numerous publications and contributions aside from what appeared in this volume, are readily accessible (see *Who's Who in Economics*). It also suffices to say that two of these academic economists are Nobel Laureates in economics: Paul Samuelson and James Buchanan. Richard Musgrave, in the words of his colleagues, should have received the Nobel. Likewise, it was said that the Nobel Prize should have been awarded to Gordon Tullock as he has coauthored *The Calculus of Consent*, which was cited among Buchanan's achievements for the award.

The Nobel Laureates in Economics

The history of contributions to the science of economics clearly demonstrates the richness of the science. Not to be overlooked is the development of ideas and models throughout the history of the Nobel awards. Glimpsing the field of research, both theoretical and empirical, from 1969-2012, one cannot but notice how the economic environment had influenced the choice of the Nobel Committee as to the subject of economics that earned the contributor the prize, but also the analytical framework that was developed to address the issue for which the prize committee has settled on. A few examples underscore this point:

Going back to the first award in 1969, the choice of the Nobel Committee for the Nobel Laureate in economics may have been influenced in their decision as to whether economics should indeed be recognized as a science. As quoted earlier in the volume, a science is one that offered hypotheses that utilized scientific methods to test those hypotheses. Over the period 1969-1973 the committee had awarded the prize to contributions that had relied on mathematical modeling and empirical analyses to describe economic relations and to provide a scientific test of the maintained hypotheses. As economics became recognized as a science in the scientific community, the Nobel Prize went to contributions made in a wide range of topics. Table A.7.1 in the Appendix to the chapter gives a chronology of the awards over the period 1969-2012.

In every year when the prize was awarded, the Nobel Laureate was cited for his (or her) contribution to the science of economics. The contributions that are recognized by the Nobel Committee, as deserving of the most coveted award are, for the most part, technical in nature. Few contributions selected have dealt with issues pertaining to the public economy, the exceptions being Buchanan's award (1986) for his development of the "contractual and constitutional bases of the theory of economic and political decision making" (see chapter 6, this volume).

It may be of interest to readers to know that almost if not all recipients of the Nobel Prize in economics are (or were) in academia. As academics, they teach (taught) economics to generations of students, and research issues to further our understanding of the working of the economic system. Their contributions have advanced concepts, ideas and methods for testing the validity of economic concepts and theories. Moreover, they are credited for developing the appropriate framework for analyzing and/or predicting the behavior of economic agents as they pursue their self-interest, or the interests of the collectivity.

Of note is the development of experimental economics where the science of economics took on a "human face" through the analysis in a laboratory type environment, the behavior of the individual as he is confronted with alternative choices. This field of study although originated at the University of Michigan in the 1950s by a psychologist, professor Ward Edward, but it was not until the year 2002 that the Nobel Committee recognized this line of inquiry by awarding the Nobel Prize to Vernon Smith, who shared the recognition and the prize with Daniel Kahneman. The prize was given in recognition of their work in integrating in the economic science insights gained from psychological research about human motivations.

While walking through the Bank of Sweden Nobel archive housing all pertinent information on the past forty-five Nobel awards, one is struck by the diversity of subjects as well as the advances made by economists in a relatively short time—less than one half a century. The discipline's fathers, from Adam Smith to Alfred Marshall did indeed make economics a science; they have labored to show would-be economists how the "world turns," although their labor was somewhat forgotten, as the discipline took on a life of its own.

A careful look at the contributions for which the Nobel Prizes were awarded would convey not only the dramatic shift in emphasis, but also the sophistication in the methods of analysis. A twentieth or a twenty-first century economist, who teaches, does research, and writes on the subject of economics, would hardly be versed in the classics at the exclusion of the new methods and advances made in the science of economics. Indeed, without the gained knowledge through the contributions of twentieth century economists, the economist would not likely to have a place in the "sun"; or for that matter in the "shade".

Of the classical economists of the eighteenth and nineteenth centuries, perhaps Leon Walras would have been as comfortable with the development of the science as those who have made their mark on the science. The use of mathematics and mathematical modeling was instituted and argued for by Walras. Today, a student in economics need not write a word of English if he can express his thought and economic learning and thesis in the language of mathematics.

The heavy reliance on the use of mathematics and mathematical modeling in economics to explain economic actions does not obscure the fact that the framework remains an economic framework. What has changed is not the questions for which the science seeks answers but the techniques that are employed to uncover those answers. In this twenty-first century and in succeeding ones, the economist would still be addressing the same old problem that has faced economists of past centuries. The difference most likely will be in the way the economist approaches the problem and the techniques he employs to reach the answer.

It is worth noting that the science of economics relies on other disciplines to enrich its contents and methods. Political science, psychology, history, and sociology are disciplines that offer insights about the behavior of man in a social setting. Economics and economists cannot but be apprised of what these disciplines have to offer and integrate the relevant teachings of these disciplines in the study of economics.

Looking back to the history of economic thought, one recognizes that the science of economics without a doubt has advanced beyond what the economists of the seventeenth, eighteenth, and nineteenth centuries had envisaged, but so have the issues confronting the individual and his nation. To be sure, not all twentieth century ideas and theories advanced by the science of economics are as simple or as enlightening as those principles set forth by the classical and neoclassical economists. Nonetheless, one needs to recognize that not all of the twentieth century problems are those of centuries past, and that the tools at the economists' disposal, by virtue of their existence, necessitate a different way at approaching the solutions.

The Economist as Adviser to Policy Makers

President Truman was quoted as saying: "give me a one arm economist". This saying reflects the economist or at least some of the economists' insistence that the advice given should contain all of the facts. So, the practice of the economic adviser is to state an opinion on the one hand to be followed by another on the other hand.

Another indication of a diversity of opinions among political advisers is a statement once attributed to President Johnson: "If you line up economists from one end of the room to the other, you would hardly find two economists agreeing with one another." Paul Samuelson acknowledges this assessment. He wrote: "According to legend, economists are supposed never to agree among themselves. If Parliament were to ask six economists for an opinion, seven answers would come back" (*Collected Papers*, 1966, p.1623).

Differences in opinion expressed by advisers reflect the essence of the economic discipline. Most economic decisions involve questions of future magnitudes, and that most societal decisions involve ethical ends that go beyond "positive" science. As Samuelson aptly put it: "no one has yet found a crystal ball that will make the future transparent" (p.1623).

Differences of opinion among political advisers moreover did not spring out of nowhere; it is perhaps the raison d'être to their proliferation. In many instances, and especially during the presidential elections in the United States, the views expressed publically and privately by political advisers echo those held by the presidential candidate and or the candidate's party.

In a society like ours, there is a line of demarcation separating two groups of advisers—those who aspire to gain influence and thus help shape the economic policy of the party in office. The second group aspires to discredit the policy of the party in power. The academic economist may get in the fray, either supporting through his research and publications or through the media the views of one group or the other. The academic economist, in arguing for one position at the exclusion of another, does so by relying on economic fundamentals to support his case. He may or may not succeed in shaping public policy, but most often gives the adviser food for thought.

The United States is a country with a two-party system, where political advisers align themselves with one party or the other. This is not the case where there exists multiparty system with different political-economic agenda.

The issues the political adviser is keen to address are as old as the age of the economic science. They cluster around two competing ideology and economic philosophy. One is "laissez faire" or "free enterprise"; the other is a capitalist system but with a "visible hand" of government.

The science of economics as outlined in the previous chapters of this volume laid down the foundations for the functioning of a market economy, and the rules that govern the individual behavior in a collective setting. The science of economics does not belong to one group at the exclusion of others. As a science, it contributes to our understanding of the conduct of individuals and business firms as they face economic decisions. It is not a handbook that one can consult to find the answer to the economy's problems.

The economist through his knowledge of his discipline relies on the scientific knowledge he has gained to address the problems he faces or posed to him. It comes as a surprise to no one that economists, although of one mind with respect to the basic principles of economics (i.e. when the supply of a good diminishes and the demand does not fall price rises), do hold different views about issues that involve moral or social judgments. In these areas the science of economics, if not silent, leaves a great deal of interpretation or misinterpretation. An example is the redistribution of income and wealth. Economists hold different views on this issue, hence one is likely to find a political adviser advocating redistribution as a means of achieving fairness, whereas another political adviser labeling such idea as an infringement on the rights of the individual. The science of economics has shied away from injecting moral judgment about one set of social policy vis-à-vis another. What wins the day is the eloquence of the policy adviser and his ability to convince the policy maker and the electorates, within the democratic framework of the superiority of the choice.

The same is true when it comes to the distribution of tax burdens. As was discussed earlier in this volume (chapter 6), the principles of taxation set forth by the classical economists, although they have remained at the foundation for tax policy, neither then nor now has the distribution of the tax burden issue been settled. To advocate a progressive or a proportional tax, one needs to know the shape of the income utility function of individuals. Although economists do assume the utility function to be declining, income utility falls as income rises, there is no solid evidence to support it, hence the differing views that are held by political advisers.

In short, political advisers hold diverse views that reflect the ambiguities surrounding issues for which the science of economics has failed to provide conclusive evidence (theoretically or empirically). Economists of all political leanings are of one mind, for example, about the futility of rent control or agricultural subsidies (although they have yet to succeed in eliminating them), but they do hold divergent views about the distribution of income, the taxation of income from capital, and on the type and level of public sector's activities. Therein lay differences in the political advice and the emergence of the political adviser.

Divergence of opinions held by political advisers is pronounced during periods of unemployment, inflation, and economic slowdown, but much more so when the level of government debt held by the public exceeds the level that is compatible with sound fiscal policy (economists seem to agree that such level should not exceed 60 percent of gross domestic product). The split in the camp of advisers becomes more visible when the President belongs to one party and the majority either in the House or the Senate from another. In such circumstances, what gets done depends on the effectiveness of the policy adviser in convincing the policy maker in either the executive branch or in congress of the soundness of his advice, even when such advice is not shared by the majority in the economic profession.

The Politics of Economics

Political advisers of different persuasions hold divergent views about economic theory and its application to public policy. Back in the 1930s there was a sharp division among advisers about the Keynesian remedy to the unemployment problem. Some advisers today still reject the Keynesian policy; others, notably Nobel laureate Paul Krugman, argue for the Keynesian approach to solve the current unemployment problem. Back in the 1980s during the Reagan era, "supply side" economics was all the rage.[2]

Not only do political advisers hold divergent views about solutions to economic problems, but academic economists also differ in their approaches to economic problems. The manifestation of what appears to the ordinary citizen as a failure of the science of economics to address problems confronting his community and country is understandable. But science, especially social science is slave to the whims of individuals.

As far back as the early nineteenth century, a bitter dispute over the Corn Laws erupted between Robert Malthus and David Ricardo lasting thirteen years. For those unfamiliar with the controversy, the Corn Laws, which existed in Britain, were protectionist laws that sheltered Britain corn producers from competition from growers of corns in the continent. Malthus was for protecting British producers of corn—the landlords. Ricardo was for free trade, that is, for abolishing all restrictions on importation of corn.

You might falsely assume that this is a simple matter. The Corn Laws were debated in Britain; position papers were written and testimonies made before the parliament over a long period of time. The Ricardo view won the day; free trade would prevail over protection. Yet, it took thirty years to achieve this outcome.

---

[2]   Krugman in his recent book *The Return of Depression Economics and the Crisis of 2008* (2009), argues that depression economics has returned. Not unlike Keynes, he believes that insufficient private demand for goods and services have become clear reasons for the global economic slowdown. For a few decades, economists ignored and drifted away from the demand side of the market, and the emphasis on the supply side of the market grew. According to Krugman, wages and prices do not respond quickly in the face of recession, and unemployment and deficient demand problems persist. Hence, the old-fashioned demand side economics still has a lot to offer. Keynesian demand policies are needed to deal with the state of economic downturn.

The resolution to the Corn Laws did indeed support the economist's long held view that gains are to be reaped through free trade rather than protection of domestic agriculture and industry. An overwhelming majority of economists today are of this view. It is not always the case that the logic of economic theory carries the day.

A fundamental, yet unresolved economic principle, involves the choice of budget posture. Economists, especially political advisers, hold very divergent views about the type and extent of several budget expenditures, tax policy, tax rates and tax bases, the distribution of tax burden, as well as the level of the public debt. One needs go no further than the current debacle over the levels of deficits in the United States and several members of the European Union to appreciate the problem facing not only political advisers, but also the economics profession as they seek resolution to these vexing problems.

To appreciate the problem, as well as the policy options advocated by the political advisers, it is perhaps useful to put the current debate over policy options in some historical perspective.

Recall the debates that were waged during the US presidential elections in the not-too-distant past:

> The next president of the United States will face pressing questions of federal budget policy. There is first, the immediate problem of ensuring that the posture of the budget—provides for an orderly continuation and completion of the recovery—. The question of how this should be accomplished has become a major public issue. Administration spokesmen stress the need for restraint in federal spending—, whereas the presidential candidate's advisers argue that the budget restraints advocated by the administration might choke the recovery" (*quotes from David Ott, et al: Nixon, McGovern and the Federal Budget, American Enterprise Institute, Washington D.C. September, (1972)*).

In the twenty-first century, the views expressed by political advisers are remarkably similar to those expressed during the 1970s. The difference between then and now is that, back then, a Republican

President was in office and was being challenged by a Democratic presidential candidate. The position was reversed in 2012, where a Democrat President was being challenged by a Republican candidate.

The advice given by the political adviser today is no different from what was advocated back in the 1970s. Back then the advisers to Nixon argued for reducing the size of the federal budget by cutting spending programs, as well as tax rates, especially for higher income groups, whereas the McGovern advisers argued for maintaining the level of federal spending to avoid a slowdown in the level of economic activity. During the Reagan presidency, supply side economists argued for spending cuts to stimulate the economy.[3]

In the 2012 presidential election, these divergent positions were voiced by the political advisers. However, with an unsustainable budget deficit, there appears to be a modicum of agreement among the political advisers about the need for some spending cuts as well as restructuring the federal tax system to rein in both the budget deficit and the federal debt.

The debate within the Euro Zone mimics what is going on in the United States; the difference is that the state of budget debt differs among members. Add to that the gap that exists between members not only in the size of debt and deficit in relation to GDP but also the level of unemployment in particular the unemployment of the young groups, which makes it more difficult to devise a unique solution to the budgetary problems.

A common problem among the US and the Euro Zone countries impacting the policy debate is the ever growing older population—in particular the impact of their health and pension needs on the national budget. There and in the United States, the fundamentals are the same. Budget allocation, especially when spending cuts are contemplated, pits the interests of the old against those of the young.

---

[3]   Arthur Laffer was one of those referred to as "supply-side" advisers. In a recent book co-authored with Stephen Moore (2011), *Return to Prosperity: How America can regain its Economic Superpower Status*, Laffer argues that "growth and prosperity circle around less regulation, and more economic freedom". He believes that they are the forces, which can turn the economy around from a state of economic decline and poverty to a state of growth and prosperity.

In the twenty-first century political advisers have to come to grips with this issue as the policy advocated regarding cutting the elder population's benefits, such as pension and medical care may not be easy, and moreover it can go part way but not by much.

In addition to advice offered in regard to the US federal budget posture, there arose an issue in the 2012 presidential election that seldom surfaces in presidential contests. This issue has to do with the distribution of power in a federal fiscal system. The United States is a federal system with three levels of governments: federal, state and local. The division of responsibilities in the US system is defined by the US Constitution, and the US Supreme Court interpretations of the US Constitution's provisions.

Article 1, section 8 of the Constitution assigns the federal government its responsibilities; the states' and local governments' functions are deemed residual. The Tenth Amendment to the US Constitution reserves to the states those powers that are not granted to the federal government or prohibited to the states (for more details on fiscal federalism, see Ott, D. and Ott, A. [1977] and Ott. A. [1993]).

The assignment of functions and hence states' rights versus federal powers surfaced in the 2012 controversy over the so-called "Obamacare" mandate. The debate highlighted the difficulties associated with the interpretation of constitutional powers of the federal government versus its subordinates; the state and local governments.

When a challenge to the federal powers is pursued, the challenge as dictated by the Articles of the Constitution is to be resolved by the Court. The Obamacare law may be viewed as a test of the powers granted by the US Constitution to the federal government versus those of the states. The decision of the US Supreme Court (June 28, 2012) with respect to the challenge to the Obamacare law did affirm the powers of the federal government in a federal fiscal system. The Obamacare law was allowed to stand.

Anyone who followed the debate over the Obamacare plan is likely to have been apprised about the sharp division of opinions expressed by the political advisers over the law. Although the majority of advisers in one camp or the other held views, either for or against this law, the opinions expressed did not quite agree with most economists' views about the role of the government. In each adviser's camp, the free market group, and those who advocate a positive role of government, especially in the provision of "merit" goods, there was some descent.

The issue is not only an issue of the federal versus the states' powers, but also about the underlying philosophy, which allows for the infringement of the sovereign over his subjects. True, there exists a great deal of infringement of both federal and state powers over the ordinary life of the individual. Many state governments in the US mandate seatbelts, car insurance, immunization, speed limits, and the like; the federal government mandates exposure to security machines, compulsory education of children up to the ninth grade, as well as the "Patriot Act," which allows the federal government to retain individuals without due process, hence violating individual rights that are also granted by the US Constitution. Yet, such rules and regulations have rarely been challenged, and when they were, the challenge has rarely reached the US Supreme Court.

Why then all the fury over the Obamacare law? The economic adviser, especially one who does not favor the Obamacare law, independent of whatever camp he belongs to, has to grapple with economic principles that would either sanction the act or refute it. The underlying philosophy of economic science for accepting or rejecting the "sovereign" infringements on individuals' rights is what economists refer to as "externality" or "third party" effect.

Take the case of the states' laws about speed limits and or not texting while driving, immunization of school children, and so forth. Laws here are not merely enacted to protect the individual subject to these restrictions, but rather to protect a "third party" from harm inflicted upon it by the actions of others.

For example, when an accident occurs that causes harm to a person (or persons) other than the driver of the car, a third party suffers from the action of another. By mandating speed limits, the government is addressing the protection of the third party. Few economists would take issue with such a mandate, although some economists might view it as infringement on individual rights.

Similarly, the argument is made for the compulsory vaccination of school age children. Given that many infectious diseases are transmitted airborne, the protection of the third party is the reason d'être for compulsory vaccination. In short, many laws (mostly at the state's level) address the third party spillovers.

At the federal level, there are laws that go unchallenged (at least did not warrant a Supreme Court ruling). Take the case of compulsory education. Education to be sure, falls in the "merit" good category; hence public money and mandates ensure that a young person receives decent level of education. The underlying philosophy is that a better-educated public makes better voters, and good education translates into good skills, which benefits society as a whole. The question that some may be asking: how does the Obamacare fit in this philosophy? That is, what third party effect would the law address?

Clearly, whether one is for the Obamacare law or against it (and there are so many details that have yet to be ironed out), the fall back has to be on the merit goods argument advanced by the traditional public economics literature.

Medical care is a good that differs from other private goods, even though the primary beneficiary is the individual receiving medical care. It is different in the same way that consumption of education differs from going to the movies or eating an ice cream cone. In both cases, education and medical care, there are spillovers—society shouldering the cost of care (under a national health insurance scheme), or partly through mandates and public expenditures (Obamacare law) society reaps the benefits from having a healthy and productive population.

At a minimum, the intent of the affirmation of the Supreme Court of the Obamacare law insures that the written article of the Constitution whereby the federal government was charged with enhancing the welfare of the citizens is upheld. The debate and the challenge to the passage of the Obamacare law will be with us for quite some time. This is for the good of the nation as it will surely determine once and for all not only what the "welfare of the citizen" entails, but also whether the way to promote the welfare is through public mandates.

Having put forth the divergent views held by economists, especially the brand of economists referred to as policy advisers, it is imperative that one acknowledges that political advisers in one camp or another do provide valuable service to those for whom they offer advice.

Political advisers not only provide policy makers with economic analyses of the issues society faces and for which the policy maker has to reach a judgment, but also educate the public at large about the implications of policy decisions advocated on their welfare. This is a valuable service that the individual seldom acquires without expending money and efforts to obtain it.

One of the drawbacks to this "democratic" dispensing of knowledge and advice has to do with the inherent characteristics of the subject of economics. In many instances, theories had to be simplified, or omitted altogether; in other times not all scientific information can be imparted to the general public. Above all most often the messenger and not the message get the attention; the analyses fall by the wayside.

Political advisers are prolific. Back in the 1950s, the 1960s and the 1970s there were few advisers to the Republican candidates for president and equally small number of political advisers to the Democratic Party candidates for president. Today, there are more advisers than there are candidates for political office.

A presidential candidate is usually advised to seek advice and tap the resources of as many advisers of the right persuasion; the challenger is also advised to do the same. With many advisers and as many divergent views about the future path of the economy, the input of any one political adviser more often than not gets a limited airing—his views may or may not be heeded.

The political adviser, unlike the political economist may dispense his advice in his capacity as a consultant or adviser, and not as a government employee. His advice may be listened to, espoused, or rejected. There is nothing that binds him to those to whom he offers his advice. The adviser could be paid a consulting fee, or he may offer his advice without being solicited for it. Media attention may be a sufficient return; the return may be in the form of book sales, television interviews, or press coverage of whatever the adviser had to impart to the general public.

In most presidential elections in the United States, a presidential candidate usually surrounds himself with a group of advisers (academic economists as well as political advisers) and, if successful, one or more of those advisers most often would be nominated for political appointment in the new administration. When this happens, the political adviser morphs into a political economist.

Paul Samuelson dispenses his advice to politicians and would be politicians: "The leaders of the world may seem to be led around through the nose by their economists' advisers. But who is pulling and who is pushing?—he who picks his doctor from an array of competing doctors is in a real sense his own doctor. The prince often gets to hear what he wants to hear." (*Collected Scientific Papers*, Samuelson, 1966, p.1515).

Summary

In our search of what economists do, one is as much bewildered about the question as about the answer. One may view the function of economists as falling along a spectrum: at one end, one finds the traditional economist, a job seeker in academia. At the other end, the political economist, who by definition has distinguished himself by being a good economist, an academic, with political acumen whose advice is sought after. Somewhere in between there is the professional economist who chooses to offer advice as a consultant to either the political establishment or the business community. In all occupations, the economist in practicing his science touches the lives of all individuals' members of his group and his society.

It is worth noting that the economist does what is expected of him. The economic discipline chartered the road that the economist is to travel. Human beings are not cut of the same cloth, so why should economists be any different?

The economist teaches principles of economics that he has learned by studying his discipline; he thinks in a structural fashion, he applies the latest research technique to understand society's problems and to develop answers to these problems. Above all what distinguishes the economist and his discipline from others is that the economist and his science continue to evolve in the search for solutions to man's survival problem.

The economist and his discipline have gone far since Adam Smith's *Inquiry into the Wealth of Nations*. He has yet a further road to travel.

8 CONCLUSIONS

This volume is about the economist and his discipline. In answering the question posed: "What Economists do, we had to elicit the answer from a review of the contributions made by the forefathers of the science of economics. Have there not been such contributions, the discipline would have not been born; economists would have been without a home.

The review took us back to the beginning, when the *Wealth of Nations* took center stage in the annals of political economy. There were to be sure "economic" concepts and ideas that were put forth by notable men of the sixteenth and the seventeenth centuries, perhaps earlier, yet for the many in and out of the discipline the birth of the science of economics has to await the emergence of economic thought put forth by an eighteenth century philosopher-political economist by the name of Adam Smith. Smith's *An Inquiry into the Wealth of Nations,* by any standard one may choose to apply, clearly defines the economist and the subject of economics.

Three centuries later, the science of economics has changed dramatically, that one would hardly recognize Smith's forest from the newcomer's tree. Yet modern day economics has retained the essence of what economics is about as postulated by our forefathers: Smith, Ricardo and Marshall to name a few. The classical economists, as well as the neoclassical economists of the past three centuries have laid a solid foundation upon which the subject of economics developed and prospered.

To define the economist on the basis of his discipline, one needs to inquire about the discipline—what it imparts and the knowledge it has accumulated. This, then, is what we have done—to define the economist, we had to journey through the history of economic thought.

Keeping in mind that today's students of economics identifies economics by its two subdivisions, micro and macro, in this volume, our journey through the history of economic thought divides the subject matter into principles that govern the behavior of the micro economy and those principles that dealt with the macro economy. This was, in a way, how economic principles have developed.

Prior to the publication in the twentieth century of Keynes's *The General Theory*, the subject of economics dealt exclusively with the conduct of individuals as consumers and producers in the market economy. Political economists were concerned with the individual action in the market place or the micro side of the discipline. Keynes brought into focus the "macro" side of the economy in his analysis of the determination of aggregate magnitudes and the failure of the invisible hand to secure for all times the full employment of society's resources as well the maintenance of price stability.

To explore with the reader how the history of economic thought has come into being and what has transpired throughout the centuries, we thought it useful to begin with some definitions. Chapter 2 defines the subject of economics. Chapter 3 tackles a critical and a controversial issue: whether economics is or is not a science. This is a thorny issue that many social scientists then and now are of two minds about. This is indeed the case, in view of the fact that of the various social science disciplines, only economics won the prize, through the recognition of the Nobel Prize Committee back in 1965.

We lay out the foundations of the discipline in chapters 4, 5 and 6. Chapter 4 deals with the principles of the micro economy, whereas chapter 5 is devoted to the macro economy. Because of the principles of economics favored the micro side of the economy, the presentation in this chapter, although quite long, does not by any mean exhaust the knowledge gained from the writing of the political economists of the eighteenth and nineteenth centuries. Nonetheless the essence of the micro relationships has been laid out adequately in the chapter.

For the macro economy, the analyses presented in chapter 5 were limited to the theories put forth by John Maynard Keynes in his *General Theory*.

Chapter 6 was devoted to the public economy. There, we present the principles that were postulated by the classical and neoclassical economists for the conduct of government. Those principles, the tax principles in particular were basically put forth as a blueprint to guide the sovereign as he pursues needed resources to carry out the state's function. The modern analysis of taxation and public expenditures as developed by Richard Musgrave and Paul Samuelson complements the early theories of taxation presented in the chapter. The modern analysis of the public economy not only provides insights on public sector functions but also addresses the issue of the optimal level of public spending. In the last section of this chapter we put forth the basic tenant of the public choice theory of the public economy as articulated by James Buchanan and Gordon Tullock in their volume *The Calculus of Consent*.

Having established in our historical journey what ideas economists espouse and advocate, we turn to the question of what economists do. Chapter 7 makes a valiant attempt at answering the question.

It is to be emphasized at this juncture, that essence of the discipline from infancy to maturity lies in formulating the principles of the private economy. As stated above, we put forth in chapter 4 the foundations of the private economy and the principles that govern human motivations and actions in the private market economy beginning with our first economist: Adam Smith. What followed in the nineteenth and twentieth centuries has been a plethora of ideas, theories, and postulates that reinforced some of Smith's principles and modified or discarded others. New ideas were put forth replacing old ones and new tools of analyses, especially "mathematics" and "econometrics" were introduced to the discipline of economics.

A student of the history of economic thought will readily recognize that the principles of the private economy put forth by Smith, Malthus, Ricardo, Walras, Mill, and Marshall could not possibly have been condensed to fit into one chapter; even if we could, it would have taxed the ability and the interest of the reader.

To guard against this tendency, we have limited the presentation to those concepts and principles that conveyed the essence of the philosophy of a market economy. To do so, we have selected from each author's volume those chapters that in our views articulated the fundamentals of a market economy and governed individual actions. The topics selected correspond to what students of economics would readily recognize as the foundations of micro analyses. Hence, the subject matter of chapter 4 is about the determination of value in exchange as it gives rise to demand prices; remunerations of agents of production as given rise to supply. These two elements constitute what we commonly discuss as the market forces, the demand and supply for both goods and factors.

The presentation in this chapter of the micro economy followed the historical development of such concepts as value, rent, wages, and profits. In doing so, our purpose was not simply to put forth what has by now become familiar to every student of economics, but rather to highlight the development of such familiar concepts. Another objective in the chronology of ideas is to showcase the contributions of individual economists in the development of such basic economic concepts; most of us students of economics take for granted. The only regret we had is that the historical review had to be limited in scope and depth. Hopefully what we have included will whet the appetite of students of economics to learn more about the foundations of the theories of the micro economy.

The other side of the economy is the behavior of its macro variables. There, the subject matter dealt with the determination of the "aggregate" magnitudes, such as national income, employment, and the price level. The study of the behavior and the determination of these variables is what commonly referred to as macroeconomics. Chapter 5 is devoted to this analysis, and by design is limited to a presentation of the macro foundations of an economy as laid out in Keynes's *The General Theory of Employment, Interest and Money*.

Although the subject of macroeconomics has undergone a great deal of reformulation since the Keynesian theory, no student of economics then or now would not recognize the path breaking achievement of the *General Theory* in laying down as well as articulating the factors that derive the aggregate economy. Advances in the study of the macro economy are numerous; sometimes the findings are contradictory, with a great deal emphasis on mathematical modeling and empirical simulation of macroeconomic policies. The testing of models and hypotheses, clearly offers insights into the behavior of macro variables as well as the effectiveness of public policy.

Since our concern in this volume was in highlighting the contributions of the founding fathers to the study of the discipline of economics, limiting the analyses to the Keynesian theory in the study of the macro economy, was in our view sufficient for that purpose.

Needless to say, that the presentation of the principles that govern the macro economy presented in chapter 5 was intended to acquaint the reader with the fundamentals of the working of the aggregate economy and how a market system may fail (often does) to provide full employment and when it actually fails, what can be done about it.

Chapter 6 first lays out principles of the public economy. This presentation is likely to be of much interest to readers, as they see themselves not interacting individually in the market economy, but interacting with others in collective action. The literature presented in the chapter put forth principles that govern or should govern the behavior of the public economy in a democratic setting. It deals with the role of government as provider of "public" and "merit" goods, its power to tax and the allocation of tax burden.

From the classical economists to twentieth century economists, we look at the budgetary choices of the state, the allocation of resources between the public and the private sectors, the provision of public and merit goods, as well as the allocation of tax burdens. The analysis presented covers tax theories advanced by the classical economists and modified by twentieth century economists. Richard Musgrave and Paul Samuelson's views about the public economy, particularly the allocation of society resources between the two sectors frame the question of how the state should interact with individuals in a democracy.

The political economy of the public sector is clearly a study of collective action within a democratic framework. To deal with this issue we have relied heavily on the thesis advanced by Buchanan and Tullock in their seminal work, *The Calculus of Consent*. There, the concept of the state and what the state does or ought to do differs significantly from the postulates advanced by Musgrave and Samuelson, regarding the role of the state. To Buchanan and Tullock, the individual acting to maximize self-interest will voluntarily behave in conjunction with his fellows in the community to maximize his welfare and the welfare of the group.

Although the public choice thesis of Buchanan and Tullock offers a distinct view and representation of the state and individuals as they interact in the public economy, it does not supplant the traditional analysis of the public sector. If anything, it enhances our knowledge of the economics of the public economy and the role of the individual as the decision maker in a free society.

Chapter 7 addresses the question posed in the title of this volume. To connect the presentation in chapter 7, "What Economists Do," with the subject matter of economics, as laid out in the previous six chapters, our journey through the history of economic thought opened for us the doors to discover what we economists actually do.

From the writing of eighteenth and nineteenth centuries, from Adam Smith to John Maynard Keynes, Richard Musgrave, Paul Samuelson Gordon Tullock, and James Buchanan, we have been apprised of the fact that economists of today are no different from those of yesterday. Each and every one seeks knowledge and dispenses knowledge for the sole purpose of enriching the life of the individual and his nation.

Our journey through the history of economic thought made it possible for us to understand as well as impart to our readers what economists actually do and/or aspire to do. Without such a journey it would have been difficult to put down or articulate what function we economists perform.

The journey, beginning with the classical economists and ending with the twentieth-century economists made it possible to articulate the principles of economics that guide the behavior of individuals in the private economy, as well as the behavior of those who are governed and those who govern in the public economy. In both economies, the economist is there not simply as an observer, but as an active participant. By observing the actions of the individual, he is able to formulate theories that explain the behavior thus observed and on the basis of such understanding, the economist is able to fashion policies that enhance individual choice and guide public actions to achieve the maximum welfare of the individual.

It is by no means certain that the economist has been or will always be successful in his endeavors, or that his accomplishments in this regard should be taken as *faits accomplis*. Rather as Alfred Marshall put it more than a century ago: "The Economist is an idea man—he acts as a servant to the state, giving advice about what function(s) it should provide,—and above all how to enrich the life of its citizens."

The economist, as political adviser dispenses advice. This, however, does not guarantee that his advice is always sound, or that his advice will always be taken. But economists are a persistent breed; they observe, analyze, and test their theories. They revise them if they must and disseminate their findings, through all forms of media, so that they will reach the various segments of society.

As a scholar, the economist performs this function well. Through his teaching, research, and publications, he spreads the gospel of economics. As our journey clearly indicates, the economist seeks to develop principles that explain the behavior of the individual, since the individual actions and motivations define the core of the private and the public economy.

The fact that the economist may be a teacher, a political economist, or a political adviser does not obscure the fact that all economists, independent of the function they perform, have one thing in common; they seek knowledge about individuals' actions as they behave individually in the market and as they behave collectively as members of a group. Understanding the behavior of individuals is a prime function of the economist.

The economist's task has and will always be one that is concerned with the behavior of both the individual and the state. His function is to understand those agents as they act in the economy, to understand the makings of a market economy as well as the alternatives to the market economy. It is not enough to praise one form of organization without knowledge of the alternatives. Therein lies the value of those principles set forth by the discipline's forefathers, for without their insights about the behavior of individuals in their capacities as consumers or agents of production, it would have been neither possible nor fortuitous to talk about the merits of one form of organization vis-à-vis another.

When everything is said and done, the ultimate answer to the question of what economists do is to state that the economists are teachers; they have taught past generations as they are teaching current generations, and hopefully future generations.

Economists have taught past generation as they are currently teaching present (and hopefully) future generations. They teach the working of the economy, especially the market economy. They have been and shall continue to be advisers to policy makers. They are scientists whose laboratory is the market place; their subject is the individual.

The economist's task is a difficult one, often impossible. Yet he is seldom discouraged, for he seeks and dispenses knowledge about man's aspirations for his welfare, the welfare of his group and his society.

The recognition bestowed on the economist by the Nobel Prize Committee (see the appendix to chapter 7) is a testimony for the importance of what the economist does. The economist, whether he is a teacher, a political economist, or an adviser to governments or businesses, is truly an idea man. Sometimes he is right, sometimes he is wrong, but right or wrong his ideas endure, his motives are pure. For him, the individual rights are supreme.

APPENDIX

Table A.7.1. The Nobel Prize in Economics: Chronology of Awards and Subjects' Contributions (1969-2012)		
Year	Laureates	Subject
1969	Ragnar Frisch and Jan Tinbergen	Dynamic Models for the Analysis of Economic Processes
1970	Paul A. Samuelson	Static and Dynamic Economic Analysis
1971	Simon Kuznets	Empirical and Theoretical Analysis of Economic Growth and the Process of Development
1972	Sir John R. Hicks and Kenneth J. Arrow	General Economic Equilibrium and Welfare Economics
1973	Wassily Leontief	The Input-Output Analysis
1974	Gunnar Myrdal and Friedrich A. Von Hayek	The Theory of Money and Economic Fluctuations and the Interdependence of Economic and Institutional Phenomena
1975	Leonid Vitaliyevich Kantorovich and Tjalling C. Koopmans	The Theory of Optimum Allocation of Resources
1976	Milton Friedman	Consumption Theory, and Functions and Stabilization Policy
1977	Bertil Ohlin and James E. Meade	The Theory of International Trade and Capital Movements
1978	Herbert A. Simon	The Decision Making Process Within Economic Organizations

1979	Theodore W. Schultz and Sir Arthur Lewis	Economic Development, With Particular Applications to Developing Countries
1980	Laurence R. Klein	Econometric Modeling and Their Applications to the Analysis of Economic Fluctuations and Economic Policy
1981	James Tobin	The Analysis of Financial Markets and Their Relations of Expenditure Decisions, Employment, Production and Prices
1982	George J. Stigler	Analysis of Industrial Structures, Functioning of Markets and Causes and Effects of Public Regulations
1983	Gerard Debreu	The Theory of General Equilibrium
1984	Sir Richard Stone	The Development of Systems of National Accounts
1985	Franco Modigliani	The Analyses of Saving and Financial Markets
1986	James M. Buchanan	The Development of the Contractual and Constitutional Bases for the Theory of Economic and Political Decision-Making
1987	Robert M. Solow	The Theory of Economic Growth
1988	Maurice Allais	The Theory of Markets
1989	Trygve Haavelmo	The Probability Theory Foundations of Econometrics and the Analysis of Simultaneous Economic Structures
1990	Harry M. Markowitz, Merton M. Miller, and William F. Sharpe	The Theory of Financial Economics
1991	Ronald H. Coase	The Significance of Transaction Costs and Property Rights for the Institutional Structure and the Functioning of the Economy
1992	Gary S. Becker	The Analysis of Human Behavior and Interaction, Including Non-market Behavior
1993	Robert W. Fogel and Douglass C. North	The Application of Economic Theory and Quantitative Methods to the Study of Economic and Institutional Change

1994	John C. Harsanyi, John F. Nash, and Reinhard Selten	Analysis of Equilibria in the Theory of Non-cooperative Games.
1995	Robert Lucas	The Hypothesis of Rational Expectations
1996	James A. Mirrlees and William Vickrey	The Economic Theory of Incentives Under Asymmetric Information.
1997	Robert C. Merton and Myron S. Scholes	Determining the Value of Derivatives
1998	Amartya Sen	Welfare Economics
1999	Robert A. Mundell	The Analysis of Monetary and Fiscal Policy Under Different Exchange Rate Regimes and the Analysis of Optimum Currency Areas
2000	James J. Heckman and Daniel L. McFadden	Theory and Methods for the Analysis of Selective Samples; Theory and Methods for the Analysis of Discrete Choice
2001	George A. Akerlof, A. Michael Spence, and Joseph E. Stiglitz	The Analysis of Markets with Asymmetric Information
2002	Daniel Kahneman and Vernon L. Smith	Experimental Economics as a Tool in Empirical Economic Analysis
2003	Robert F. Engle and Clive W. J. Granger	Analysis of Economic Time Series with Common Trends (co-integration)
2004	Finn E. Kydland and Edward C. Prescott	Dynamic Macroeconomics: The Time Consistency of Economic Policy and the Driving Forces Behind Business Cycles
2005	Robert J. Aumann and Thomas C. Shelling	The Analysis of Conflicts and Cooperation in Game Theory
2006	Edmund S. Phelps	Analysis of Intertemporal Tradeoffs in Macroeconomic Policy
2007	Leonid Hurwicz, Eric S. Maskin, and Roger B. Myerson	The Foundations of Mechanism Design Theory
2008	Paul Krugman	The Analysis of Trade Patterns and Location of Economic Activity
2009	Elinor Ostrom and Oliver E. Williamson	Analysis of Economic Governance

2010	Peter A. Diamond, Dale T. Mortensen and Christopher A. Pissarides	Analysis of Markets with Search Frictions
2011	Thomas J. Sargent and Christopher A. Sims	Empirical Analysis of Cause and Effect in the Macro Economy
2012	Alvin E. Roth and Lloyd S. Shapley	The Theory of the Stable Allocation and the Practice of Market Design

BIBLIOGRAPHY

Buchanan, James, and Tullock, Gordon. 1965. *The Calculus of Consent: Logical Foundations of Constitutional Democracy.* Ann Arbor Paper Books, The University of Michigan Press, Ann Arbor, Michigan.

Gide, Charles, and Charles Rist. (1915) 1948. Translated by R. Richards. *The History of Economic Doctrines.*, London: G.G, Hamp & Co.

Harberger, A., and M. Bailey, eds. 1969. *The Taxation of Income from Capital.* Washington, DC: The Brookings Institution Press.

Harris, Seymore E., ed. 1952. *The New Economics: Keynes' Influence on Theory and Public Policy.* New York: Alfred A. Knopf.

Heilbroner, Robert L. 1953. *The Worldly Philosophers: The Lives, Times and Ideas of the Great Economic Thinkers.* New York: Simon and Schuster.

Kaldor, N. 1955. *An Expenditure Tax.* London: George Allen & Unwin.

Keynes, John Maynard. (1936) 1954. *The General Theory of Employment, Interest and Money* London: Macmillan and Co.

Krugman, Paul. 2009. *The Return of Depression Economics and the Crisis of 2008.* Reprint, New York: W. W. Norton & Company.

Laffer, Arthur, and Stephen Moore. 2011. *Return to Prosperity: How America Can Regain Its Economic Superpower Status*. New York: Threshold Editions.

Lindahl, Erik. 1958. "Some Controversial Questions in the Theory of Taxation.," In *Classics in the Theory of Public Finance*, edited by Richard A. Musgrave and Alan T. Peacock, 214-232.

Malthus, Robert. (1798) 1969. *On Population*. Edited by Gertrude Himmmelfarb. New York: The Modern Library.

Mansfield, Edwin. 1974. *Economics, Principles, Problems, Decisions*. New York: W. W. Norton & Co.

Marshall, Alfred. (1890) 1948. *Principles of Economics: An Introductory Volume*. London: Macmillan & Co.

Massel, Mark. 1959. "Competition and Monopoly.," In *Economics and the Policy Maker: Brookings Lectures 1958-1959*. Washington, DC: The Brookings Institution.

Mill, J. Stuart. (1848) 1969. *Principles of Political Economy, with Some Applications to Social Philosophy*. Edited by Sir William Ashley. New York: Augustus M. Kelley Publishers.

Musgrave, Richard Able. 1959. *The Theory of Public Finance: A Study of Public Economics* New York: McGraw Hill Book Company.

Neale, Tom. 1966. *An Island to Oneself*. Woodbridge, CT: Ox Bow Press.

Nichols, Donald A., and Clark W. Reynolds. 1971. *Principles of Economics*. New York: Holt, Rinehart and Winston.

Ott, Attiat F., 1993. *Public sector budgets: A comparative study*. Aldershot, England: Edward Elgar Publishing Company.

—, 2002. *The Public Sector in the Global Economy.* Chelthenham, UK: Edward Elgar Publishing Company.

—et al., (2008), "A Tribute to Richard Abel Musgrave", Journal of Economics and Finance: 32 (4), pp.330-333.

Ott, David, et al. 1972. *Nixon, McGovern and the Federal Budget.* Washington, DC: American Enterprise Institute for Public Policy Research.

Ott, David, and Attiat Ott. 1977. *Federal Budget Policy.* Third edition, Washington, DC: The Brookings Institution Press.

Pigou, A. C. 1951. *A Study in Public Finance.* Third edition, London: Macmillan& Co.

Ricardo, David. (1817) 1952. *On the Principles of Political Economy and Taxation.* Edited by Piero Sraffa. Cambridge: Cambridge University Press.

Rogin, Leon. 1956. *The Meaning and Validity of Economic Theory: A Historical Approach.* New York: Harper & Brothers Publishers.

Samuelson, Paul A. 1938. "The Empirical Implications of Utility Analysis." *Econometrica* 6 (4): 344-356.

—. 1955. "Diagrammatic Exposition of a Theory of Public Expenditures." *The Review of Economics and Statistics*: 37 (4), pp.350-356.

—. 1958. "Aspects of Public Expenditure Theories." *The Review of Economics and Statistics* 40 (4): 332-338.

—. 1966. *The Collected Scientific Papers of Paul A. Samuelson*, vols.1 and 2. Edited by Joseph E. Stiglitz Cambridge, MA: The MIT Press.

Schumpeter Joseph. 1999. *The History of Economic Analysis*, 1994 edition; Rutledge.

Smith, Adam. (1776) 1937. *An Inquiry into the Nature and Causes of the Wealth of Nation*. The Modern Library. New York: Random House.

—. (1854) 2000. *The Theory of Moral Sentiments*. Amherst, NY: Prometheus Books.

Stigler, George J. 1965. *Essays in the History of Economics*. Chicago and London: The University of Chicago Press.

Taussig, F. W. 1926. *Principles of Economics*, vol.1. Third edition, New York: Macmillan & Co.

Von Wieser, Friedrich. 1958. "A Theory of the public Economy." In *Classics in the Theory of Public Finance*, edited by Richard Musgrave and Allen Peacock, 190-201. London: Macmillan & Co.

Walras, Leon. (1873, 1876) 1954. *Elements of Pure Economics*. Translated by William Jaffe. Published for the American Economic Association and the Royal Economic Society., Homeword, Illinois: Richard Irwin.

www.ingramcontent.com/pod-product-compliance
Lightning Source LLC
Chambersburg PA
CBHW030935180526
45163CB00002B/572